UNLEASHING
CAPACITY

THE HIDDEN HUMAN RESOURCES

RITA TREHAN

First Edition
Copyright © 2016 Rita Trehan. All rights reserved.
A catalogue record for this book is available from the British Library.

ISBN (Paperback): 978-1-911443-98-8
ISBN (Ebook): 978-1-911443-99-5

Published by Large Things Ltd.
Designed and Set by SWATT Design Ltd www.swatt-design.co.uk

Printed internationally by Ingram Spark

For more information, or to buy copies of this book please visit
www.ritatrehan.com

The HR CEO

The tools and capabilities available to today's HR professionals provide a unique position that, when used correctly, can lead to that all-important—and highly coveted—role at the leadership table. But how to get there?

Author Rita Trehan has distilled her experience as a global leader at Honeywell and AES Corporation into a series of easily digestible chapters designed to help today's HR professional attain and keep a seat at the corporate decision-making table. Trehan offers specific strategies for reframing the HR professional's understanding of their role within the company, including viewing the corporation not from the HR fishbowl, but rather from the vantage point of the CEO's office.

HR directors not only supply the human resources—they can actually drive the changes needed to propel the organization into new markets, new technology, new products, and entirely new means of operation. With the tools and framework introduced in this book, readers will be poised to gain ground within top management by constantly expanding the conversation to include winning solutions that solve their problems. They will be empowered to become the change agents needed to drive for results.

Contents

PREFACE

"IT'S TIME HR GOT A MAKEOVER"

ACKNOWLEDGMENTS

1 CAPACITY-CENTRIC HR

2 BEHIND THE SCENES NO MORE

3 BEYOND MODELS

4 THE CAPACITY FRAMEWORK

5 WANTED—CHIEF CAPACITY OFFICER

6 WIN THE GAME BY CHANGING THE GAME

7 HR'S IMAGE PROBLEM

SOME CLOSING THOUGHTS

ABOUT ME:

TESTIMONIALS

PREFACE
"IT'S TIME HR GOT A MAKEOVER"

A conversation with an HR professional

Around water coolers, break rooms, conference rooms, and in private spaces across the world, conversations are taking place between HR professionals. These conversations are tough, full of stress and despair—Let's see if this sounds familiar to you:

"What's wrong?"

"I can't stand it. I'm behind the 8-ball again." "What do you mean?"

"I just got out of a meeting after a day of trying to put out fires, and they've made another decision without me. And now I'm responsible for refocusing the team on this latest demand, so we can try to give them what they're asking for, on top of everything else we have to do. I'm really frustrated! I feel like giving up."

"That's crazy! Aren't you in the middle of a huge re-launch of the HR model?"

"Yes! And they don't care. They think it's just us tinkering with our structure again and not actually doing anything substantial. I don't know how to explain that we're already in the weeds with our own process, and now we have to take on this other crazy initiative. HR wasn't even at the table when the decision was made!"

"Wow! I can't believe they made that decision without you!" "They do it all the time. I ask to be invited to meetings, and they just ignore me. I keep building all these workbenches and performance tools, but nobody seems interested in them. They create these initiatives without me, behind closed doors. It's like they don't even care that HR is working as hard as it can. All they're interested in is that we deliver what they want. We get zero input. We're never invited to participate, even though we're major stakeholders in the outcomes."

Sound familiar?

It was conversations like this that caused me to write this book. The despairing HR professional in this example is right: His/her management team doesn't care that HR is tinkering with organization, trying to fix and reconfigure itself so its processes are perfect for the management team. They need HR to deliver on the main need of the company, which is the management of the people-resources—

According to management teams, HR executives haven't proven their worth outside the knowledge of their own products and services. They aren't at the decision-making table because they're not showing any knowledge or true interest in adding to the conversation outside of what HR is doing to improve itself.

What does this mean, exactly? They're not speaking the language of the organization. They're not using HR tools to improve the operational capabilities of the company. Without that understanding, they're merely standing outside the room, wondering why they can't be on the other side.

But there's a way to get that seat at the decision-making table. I've had that seat, and I know what it takes to get there. You need business acumen and tools that can transform your position within the organization. It doesn't matter from what level of awareness you begin. The seat at the table you desire can be yours, and I'm going to show you how to get it.

Who am I?

My name is Rita Trehan.

I've made a career of large-scale transformations within Fortune 200 companies. As a global HR leader at Honeywell and AES Corporation, I helped rethink how corporate objectives were achieved. From finding more profitable ways to launch entire divisions around the world to having created highly effective ways of measuring performance, I've taken it as my charge to deliver cutting-edge, strategic solutions in less time by focusing on actual results.

Today, I'm bringing my real-world perspective and track record of success to help organizations both large and small continue to up their game. I'm especially interested in helping people like you get the success you want through sharing what I've learned in the course of my 20+ year career as an HR executive.

It's been my experience that HR is constantly fighting for that seat at the table without being equipped to handle what the seat at the table entails.

The way to earn and keep your place at the table is to stop viewing the problem from behind the HR desk and from within the HR silo. It's time to step outside that office and view your corporation as your CEO sees it. You have to expand your mind to think like a CEO. You have to consider things outside the silo of just the tools of your trade(Talent Acquisition, Compensation/Benefits/Rewards, HR Service Centers, Organizational Design, etc.). You must begin to think how you'll apply those tools to move the company forward toward its main driver of success: increased capacity.

I have reaped the rewards of being invited into board meetings because the members believed I had much to contribute in helping the company to meet its more important goals, among them the creation of shareholder value. I've earned the respect of my peers in the C-suite through building powerful relationships and forming a powerful alliance with my CEO. I want to teach you how to do that, too. I want you to play the corporate game to win, and capacity is the way to win the seat at the table and success beyond your imagining.

Who should read this book?

If you're asking yourself the questions posited above, you are reading the right book.

Capacity is the only way companies can accomplish their goals. It's how they win in the marketplace, weather rough times, and launch business-winning initiatives that make the news. Capacity is how the work gets done and the lights stay on. The CEO is either ringing the bell at the New York Stock Exchange or turning over the keys to his office in defeat.

Whether the company has five people or fifty thousand, viewing the organization and its objectives through the lens of capacity is the only way to win. As the owner of people resources for your corporation, you ultimately own capacity for the organization, as it's those individuals and the resources surrounding them that make the difference between a company's success and failure in meeting its goals. With the tools and framework introduced in this book, you'll be uniquely poised to gain ground with your top management by constantly expanding the conversation to include winning solutions that solve their problems. When you begin working with capacity in mind, you'll be invited to every discussion because you can point out opportunities where none were previously thought to exist. I'm confident that the powerful tools in this book will rekindle your excitement about the HR field; that's what empowerment does for you. You'll be energized to make decisions. You'll rediscover your passion as you increase company value by working alongside, instead of just at the behest of, the people responsible for meeting the company's goals. You'll be invited to top meetings. The doors that were once closed will begin to open, and you'll soon be in front of your workload, instead of constantly under the gun delivering on initiatives that relegate you to mere service delivery.

Those who desire to elevate their performance as HR professionals, who wish to lead rather than be led, and who want to take their companies and careers into the next century on a wave of success— they are the audience for this book.

With capacity as a frame of reference, we will explore the exciting future not only of HR but also of the corporate world overall.

How is this book different?

I've read many supposedly game-changing books directed at transforming HR departments. When you add these to all the consultants and endless white papers and conferences, it seems as though HR delivery has been redesigned to death. As we'll discuss further in this book, it's not the model of HR that's dooming it to a merely administrative function, seen at best as an afterthought or worse a necessary evil for the company, that does no more than deliver what's demanded of it while avoiding legal and compliance trouble. The model is really the least of our concerns.

We must change the mindset through which we view our roles.

This book is not a list of suggestions of how to evolve the actual tools of Human Resources. It doesn't offer any ideas about how to win by centralizing administrative processes, nor does it speak about how to get closer to your management team by developing a new dashboard for performance management or a quick turnaround on talent reviews. This book is a tool to change the way you view how those tools work—to see that they don't just solve problems but also create opportunities. The decision-making tools and advice in this book will allow you to elevate your thought processes by constantly thinking "capacity first." By making this your primary concern, you will view all problems as a business owner and be able to create solutions that will be of great value to your C-suite clients. With this mindset, you will start to run HR like a leading corporation, and it will, in turn, start performing like one.

This is not a book about how to make HR processes better. It is a book about leadership, our conversations, and about raising our deliverables to the level of the C-suite and beyond. This is about how to deliver results worthy of that seat at the table by thinking like you're already there. This is about winning by thinking like a CEO and viewing every opportunity to do your job as a chance to practice that. You are the

CEOs of HR. With the tools in this book, I'd like to see you become the top contenders for the CEO position. It is time for corporate CEOs to rise to power through the ranks of HR.

Perhaps that person will be you.

Did you see it coming?

Everything about the world in which we work is changing. Cloud technology and social media have flattened the organization, rendering the highest levels of leadership instantly accessible without the need for the usual internal and external communication channels. New hires and recruits can speak to CEOs on Twitter, Facebook pages can be used to market corporate messages, and company information can be accessed via mobile in mere seconds. For HR professionals, the definition of "customer" has expanded: it seems everyone inside the company and a whole host of individuals externally are now our customers. International expansion has become infinitely possible with the addition of technology, which makes it easier to connect people to their world of work and to business in general, regardless of their location.

Our workplaces have also expanded to include our couches and coffee houses. In the past, we've used HR to support only the talent within skyscrapers and offices; now that we live in a world without walls, our practices need to change. We must evolve the concepts of HR practice or we will become obsolete.

View this evolution as exciting, not threatening! You are uniquely qualified to lead your company through these types of challenges, and if you're willing to let go of some old ways of thinking, you can take your career to a seat at the table and beyond. It's your ticket to the C-suite.

Are you ready to take charge of this change? I invite you on a journey to discover the tools and insights that will forever alter the course of your destiny.

Come with me into the world of capacity-driven business: the evolution of HR in the twenty-first century and beyond.

ACKNOWLEDGMENTS

There are so many people who have played an important part in my life. On the personal side, my family, of course, and my husband who, for whatever reason, believes I can do anything I put my mind to (thank you, Richard, for your never-ending support). Career-wise, so many people have been instrumental in shaping my thoughts and showing me what is possible that it is difficult to call them all out, but there are some that deserve to be called out.

To Steve Foster, whose ability for business facts and business taught me early on what it meant to be business-centric. There were others in the HR field who also did much to inspire me including Betty Bowman, Louise Holloway, and many others. To Jay Kloosterboer, a great mentor, who challenged me on a constant basis to achieve what at times I thought impossible—(Jay, who would have thought I would come to love executive compensation!) To colleagues within the HR field, there are too many to mention, but the early days at AES were special, so thanks to Lawrence LeBlanc, Louis Montgomery, John Zaranchik and Ginette Martin—we did a lot and made a lot of good things happen!

There were so many business leaders, CEOs that gave me the opportunity, and more than that influenced my understanding of business and diverse business styles. From my early career days at Honeywell, to the "Cottage Inn" group—Bob Baker, Colin Millar, and Alan Wright—I learned a lot! Gerard Goubau, you taught me a lot about business across international boundaries. Leo Quinn, you were a force of nature. Louise Overy, thank you for your early guidance.

Paul Hanrahan, Andres Gluski, Bob Hemphill, Phil Odeen, Joe Brandt, Victoria Harker, and all of the other leaders and individuals at AES, thank you for giving me the opportunity to help shape the function of HR and much, much more at AES. We may not always have seen eye to eye on everything, but that's the great thing about having a seat at the table. I was allowed to contribute and have a seat.

Andy Vesey, there are so many things I've learned over the years working with you that it's hard to pick out any single thing, but some deserve a mention. First, your vision and passion for pushing the boundaries means that people are challenged to think differently, innovatively and most importantly, push ourselves to be the best we can be.

You are also a great advocate of HR and what it can do, yet at the same time you have shown me the importance of not sitting on our laurels but constantly seeking ways to make the business better. Your leadership was an inspiration in so many ways.

Last, but not least, I have been lucky enough to see a number of talented young people go on to do great things in HR and in the business, and I want to thank them for the opportunity to work with them and see them grow. Thank you!

1
CAPACITY-CENTRIC HR
The Key to the C-suite
and Beyond

CEOs would ideally want HR leaders to not only simply understand the functions of HR, but also to understand what Marketing is doing, what Finance is up to, what Sales is achieving, and how Operations is coming along. And they want us to ask, "How can I help?"

That's company-centric HR.

Introduction

Today's corporate environment is growing and changing at a rapid pace. Opportunities abound and organizations must be agile enough to swiftly change and adapt to new market conditions and demands.

The role and personality of the CEO in today's organization is far different from the old focused, insular, "my way or the highway" mentality. The not-so-distant past saw a C-suite and senior management populated mainly by company men who ascended to the throne by attaching themselves to the right people. Collaboration and teamwork were not necessarily as important as the ability to navigate the political landscape while understanding and flawlessly executing orders.

Today's dynamic CEOs are open collaborators who run vibrant, ever-changing organizations that adapt quickly to the world marketplace. They create global teams to apply cutting- edge strategies in workplaces that exist almost exclusively in the ether of the Internet. Cloud technology is becoming central to the infrastructure of such workplaces. At the same time, consumers can touch the company directly via social media, and supply chain management can be done without much brick and mortar.

Executing strategy in this new world requires a broader, more informed view of one's company, its resources, and of the world itself. Achieving top performance now requires CEOs to rely upon advisors in many fields, each contributing more sophisticated solutions and perspectives than ever before. Each advisor is responsible for providing solutions to handle the successful operation, expansion, and profitability of their company. Although their disciplines vary, all members of this elite, decision-making force have one thing in common: they provide resources.

This book focuses on the role of the advisor responsible for resources of the human variety, a function much maligned throughout the years for its seeming inability to see outside of their department and lead strategically.

But I believe it is entirely possible for HR leaders to gain the big-picture, strategic toolset CEOs so desperately desire them to possess. This consultative agility is perfectly within the purview of the 21st century HR professional and department. It's what I like to call *capacity-centric HR*, which changes the view of the HR professional from task oriented to company focused.

What does that even mean?

In the past, HR was just a newer, fancier moniker for the personnel department. Not any more. The tools and capabilities available to today's HR professionals provide a unique position that, when used correctly, can lead to that all-important—and highly coveted—mission-critical role at the leadership table. They not only supply the human resources, but also can drive the changes needed to propel the organization into new markets, new technology, new products, and entirely new means of operation. They are uniquely positioned to be the change agents needed to drive results.

That said, there's a major paradigm shift that must happen first: they must move from their usual task orientation to a greater focus on enlarging their capabilities and achieving the results the company needs to thrive. Human Resources is really a business within a business, and it should be run as such. That's what capacity-centric HR is all about.

But what exactly is capacity-centric HR? The concept is about driving the company forward by focusing on using the tools and information at its disposal to create capacity. The more traditional HR functions and processes evolve from service delivery and performance dashboards to knowing how to combine those tools to achieve corporate objectives. Strategic HR professionals who think about things from the perspective of capacity prize the same goals and metrics as the company at large. Their mental lens zeroes in on longer-range objectives of expansion, technological advance, and global reach, and creating and maintaining the resources to meet those needs. In other words, they are focused on building the capacity needed to maintain and grow a leading-edge company.

Capacity-centric HR is concerned with whether or not an organization is capable of meeting or exceeding its strategic goals given the resources necessary to achieve them in the competitive marketplace.

It is this perspective, this consultative mindset, that HR needs to provide to senior management. And it is this advisory role, the rightful place of which is at the senior management table, that I believe we HR professionals need to embrace as the future leadership profile of our profession. We hold the keys to capacity, and within capacity lies the future of the company's success.

In this book, we'll talk about the power of capacity and its truly amazing potential to allow you to create needed changes. We love new monikers in HR, so we'll focus on one brand new title, which applies to you in particular: Chief Capacity Officer.

We'll go into this in more depth as we move forward, but the mantle of Chief Capacity Officer with a capacity-centric mindset allows you to see the differences between:

> » Being rooted in solely delivering the company's vision vs. creating that vision and leading the charge to deliver sustainable change

> » Having to work within a set strategy you had no part in creating vs. crafting and translating strategy for the C-suite, the board, and the company overall

> » Delivering packaged solutions to bring about change vs. becoming the game changer: challenging the status quo, and bravely driving the direction toward innovative solutions

> » Leading with a bias in favor of HR and its processes vs. helping to lead the company to results with a bias toward the organization

It is by approaching HR with this lens, this renewed focus on capacity, that will allow us to shift where we stand in the spectrum of value. Throughout the course of this book, we will explore the many facets and applications of this concept. Our journey will take us out of the HR silo and into every dimension of the corporation, from cutting-edge technology to emerging markets, and beyond.

But, first, let's talk about that seat at the table: ...*what exactly does that involve?*

What does it mean to be a powerful HR partner?

Depending on your organization and its opinion of HR, you either enjoy a strong partnership or a less-than-desirable position as a processing function. There seems to be a misconception that all HR is capable of achieving is just administrative in nature, when in reality the department and its leadership can lead and transform the organization in ways other departments simply can't.

We own part of this misconception.

Some big mistakes of the past have positioned HR solely as the department that deals with "people resources." We missed our opportunity in the 1990s to take to heart David Ulrich's proposal that HR needed to become a strategic business partner. Even at that time, the message from the CEO and business community was loud and clear: HR teams need to focus on meeting the needs of the business, not merely improving their own processes. Unfortunately, in trying to act on that message, we got hung up on the mechanics and continued to tinker with our organizational model; we failed to get the bigger message entirely. We've since continued to interpret the need for "HR transformation" as "transforming the HR organization model."

Here's the problem: you can have any configuration of the department you like, but if you don't understand how the marketplace has changed and adapt your decision-making models to address those changes, you'll accomplish very little— outside of sharpening the basic administrative processes and constantly moving boxes on the org chart.

Becoming a formidable HR partner and creating a strong internal organization that delivers strategic direction requires more than a new model— it calls for a new mindset.

That concept can be a bit daunting and confusing. What does that mindset involve? What does it look like?

To answer these questions, you need look no further than your CEO as an example of the leadership perspective and mindset that we must model.

If you hear the voice of the CEO in your decision making, daily thinking, and strategic direction, you will see a great evolution in your ability to make decisions from a more successful perspective—which will lead to greater personal success at the same time. I've personally had the opportunity to learn from the best. I can say that the most effective CEOs *and* CHROs (Chief Human Resources Officers) have similar traits that set them apart, and that make them destined for success in their leadership roles however much those roles may differ. While their responsibilities may differ, they embody these eight traits.

The Eight Characteristics of Top CEOs and CHROs:

1. **Analytical Prowess:** Sharp leaders have the ability to gather information without ego, to connect resources, data, and facts in order to make the right decision. They excel at marshaling resources to obtain key knowledge.

2. **Strong Intuition:** Certain things keep them up at night; they feel things at a gut level and aren't afraid to make the tough call based on hard data and the feeling that something is right. They become informed; and when the time is right, they act.

3. **Egoless Curiosity:** They want to know what they don't know, seeking experts far and wide to gain information. They have a yearning to learn. They read; they ask a lot of questions. They aren't afraid to say they don't know everything. There are few sacred cows in their minds. They're always trying to think about what comes next. They are always wondering if there's a better way to do what they're doing and if the next big thing is just around the corner.

4. **Inspiring Energy:** Their enthusiasm is infectious. They infuse excitement, drive, and determination into the entire organization. People would follow them through the gates of hell if the call were issued. They know how to motivate because they're motivated by a genuine passion.

5. **Incurable Optimism:** Top leaders have the ability to garner and create a leadership following by developing, challenging, and harnessing talent to achieve what sometimes seems impossible. "Impossible" is not in their vocabulary.

6. **Relentless Reinvention:** That passion for change pushes the envelope in generating new insights—new ways of

approaching problems—and opportunities. They remain outwardly focused with their sights set on the future without losing touch with the here and now.

7. **Lack of Fear of Failure:** Their willingness to try new things is inspirational to their teams. They are not afraid to fall down because they know the value in the lessons they'll learn. We don't learn much from easy wins; it's in failure that we take the time to reflect deeply on our actions. Effective leaders are not embarrassed by mistakes, but use the information gained from them to make sure they succeed the next time.

8. **Unwavering Self-Confidence:** Their confidence is solid as a rock, which allows their passion to bring out the best in everyone. They're never shaken because they're plugged into a constant source of inner power. They surround themselves with the best and brightest, confident in their ability to pick the right team, which they know is the secret to being a strong leader.

These leadership qualities can be found not just at the top, but can also be spotted throughout the organization. They can also—and this is the game changer—be taught and instilled in all who wish to possess them. These qualities can be used to build HR partners who can drive for results in a positive way, with an eye toward achieving the larger business objectives at hand.

The fact is that the future of thriving corporations depends upon impactful HR partners: powerful allies who can propel the business into a trajectory of success. And, you can't have HR people like that unless you cultivate them as full collaborators who share the CEO's values, perspective, and leadership qualities.

If you're a CEO, a powerful, business-savvy HR partner is invaluable. Let's take as an example the evolution and utilization of cloud-based technology in business. An impactful CHRO would be in the office of the CEO, leading the discussion about how such technology could bring increased productivity, discussing its effects on the cost model and providing hard facts about any and all impacts on headcount and the organization overall.

They would have a viewpoint on the responsibilities that must be assumed to take advantage of the evolution of technology in business. The discussion would be centered on understanding the organizational impact and leveraging technology for overall corporate improvement. Nowhere in this discussion would there be fear-based speculation about how it's going to change the HR piece of the equation.

The difference between this discussion and typical discussions about HR is that the CHRO is involved. It didn't happen in a vacuum where other C-Suite executives did all the talking about impact and made all the decisions without consulting HR. Nor was the conversation led by the Chief Technology Officer. The CHRO is part of the discussion at the start, when a CHRO can add value and contribute insight, and not at the end when the design is already figured out. They're at the right hand of the CEO, and they are seen as an invaluable voice in all decisions.

Another example is the HR partner who interacts with the board of directors, whose role it is to constantly take the temperature of those whose investments bear the brunt of the overall corporate risk. The impactful HR partner, playing the role of independent, trusted advisor, understands what the board is seeking and continually advises the CEO on how to best partner with its members. These powerful HR partners don't insist on a seat at the table; they earn their place through a track record of continual results, gained from game-winning decisions made at every opportunity—self-created or granted. Powerful CHROs do not limit their input to the parts of the discussion about people. Instead, they're invested in the decision as a whole, not just the HR component of the equation.

A powerful CHRO attends investor conferences and gets invited by the CEO to represent the company. CFOs do it; other leaders within the organization do as well, and if you have the same credibility and professional depth as those individuals, you get to be part of the big stuff: talking to investors, speaking at industry events, and demonstrating that you're immersed in the inner workings of the company. You're considered a valuable member of the leadership team and are trusted to display your knowledge at every turn.

So, let's look at this from the HR partner side of the equation. How do you know if you are, indeed, a valued ally? Outside of the examples above, how can you tell if you are in that seat at the table or standing somewhere in the vicinity? Or, in some cases, not even in the same room.

CHROs know they're considered impactful partners when they're the CEO's first sounding board, when the trust level and the value they bring to the table is indispensable. The two can have candid conversations and respectfully disagree without fear of a damaged working relationship or retribution. If you enjoy such a position, you feel confident in your ability to dissent when necessary and empowered to implement what's right for your organization.

A powerful HR partner knows conversations start with a discussion about the company, not what should be done with this person or that individual process. When you have created your Leadership Brand, when your focus is on the overall outcome of decisions for the company, when your results are tied to meeting (and exceeding) company performance metrics—these are signs that you're an impactful HR partner.

It's the difference between being in the political mix versus being outside the room listening at the door. You are not last on the list on the budget conversation, when the departments are coming to ask for support and willing to pay for it. You are leading the discussions.

You are pulling, rather than being pushed. Setting things in motion is impact; trying to handle things that are already moving without your input is not.

Reality HR, Season 1: The revamp of the company website

I was part of the review team for a corporate-wide, tactical move to revitalize the web presence of our organization. This was an interesting and important initiative for the company, and the team and I were eager to participate. The initial meeting was vital to the success of the whole project. In order to contribute effectively, I did not let my conversations become HR-centric; I focused on much broader questions: how we could learn from the experts, and which stakeholders mattered the most to the end result? Rather than create a predefined site that appealed to all, I made the case that it would be better to employ the 80–20 Rule, focusing on the audience who visited the website most. I was trying to push the envelope, questioning the return on investment of the revamp and its impact. How much would it cost to maintain? Was social media the right platform for a business like ours, etc.? At the end of the meeting, several people told me that my questions helped them think about the site from their own functional perspective. The result was that collectively we were able to view the redesign initiative from a company-wide perspective rather than from our own individual points of view. HR actively contributed to the discussion, and the initiative became a silo-breaker that was beneficial for all parties.

Reality HR, Season 2: The Strategic Business Development Council

As a senior executive, I was part of a Business Development Committee that screened and approved investments for new business. At the end of one of our Investment Committee meetings, one of the divisional presidents approached me to say that a number of his leaders asked why I was involved in the meetings, challenging my right to participate. After all, I was in HR, so why did I have a vote on whether they were given investment dollars to pursue a new project or idea? He said he told them I was not afraid to ask questions, and that my comments often provided valuable insight. I was truly grateful that he'd taken the opportunity to shift people's perspective and to champion my position.

The reality is that CHROs will face this kind of negative perception a lot. How you deal with it is important. I took every opportunity to make sure I asked questions if I didn't understand; and if I commented, it was not just for the sake of commenting, but to help the organization make the right decision.

Last, but not least, I did bring the people factor into the discussion when it was appropriate. Did we really think we have the human capacity and capability to go further into a new project? How did we think we could be successful when we knew we had struggled to get the right talent in certain positions? Were we overreaching? Were the people costs going to be significant and would they be worth the ROI?

As an example, we made some tough calls, saying no to investments in markets where we had a limited talent pool and where finding talent would be highly expensive, and challenge our cost model. The ability to raise and address these concerns made quite a difference.

True, issues like this might have been raised even if I wasn't present. But, the fact is that the people side of the equation is often overlooked in discussions about business development where high returns are at the top of the agenda. In fact, I'd like to think that my influence extended beyond this meeting. And, I think it really did, since the company decided to take things in a different direction as the result of my questioning. One of those questions was why the team thought they'd be able to deliver this specific project on time and on budget when their track record proved otherwise. Connecting past performance to future performance was critical for me, not only in assessing the depth of analysis that had gone into the deal, but also in bringing it to the forefront. As a leadership team, we were making informed decisions from a larger context and point of view.

HR must set its sights on the big picture of the company, not just on the functional details of its own department. But, that doesn't mean that the functional must be abandoned in favor of "strategy." There's a new way to look at the vital functional deliverables of HR, of which there are a great many: you must ask yourself, "What problem am I trying to resolve?" from a broader context, so that the focus is on solving the business issue. In my last major project that involved organizational transformation, we redesigned the whole Corporate Center. All corporate departments were reviewed to determine which services and solutions were to be managed at the corporate level, and which would be handled at the business level. Simply put, our efforts were focused on determining what made sense to centralize at the headquarters level and what would be devolved to the businesses.

In the initial discussions around the HR department with the Executive Team, I drove discussions from the position of what was best for the divisions, which, depending on the ultimate model selected, could also result in the elimination or reshaping of my own department. As executive leaders, our role (mine included) was to take an objective view when making decisions, even if that meant significant changes for our own stakes in the game. Performance at a C-suite level depends upon this "company first" mindset. It turned out that the HR function was not eliminated, but given an opportunity to expand and refocus. This presented a most interesting and challenging dilemma: how would we reshape all our traditional transactional services, particularly the compensation function, across multiple markets? The challenge was to view these services through a strategic lens versus just focusing on volume and standardization, which is the lens through which transformation for deliverables of this type is usually viewed.

Personally, I was quite excited by the challenge, but none of the team was chomping at the bit to take on the role. I couldn't understand it. They kept telling me that the whole thing was transactional and not strategic, but the whole point was that we had the most to gain by looking at transactions with a strategic eye. The transactional functions were actually the most strategic and impactful of all. Why? Because centralizing the day-to-day processes of the division in a single, solutions-based platform could allow it to become a solutions-driven center of excellence with the power, in turn, to impact the culture of the entire company for the better. Imagine a world where all your tools are combined to serve you in a single toolbox rather than separate boxes for each tool. Exciting, right? We proceeded with that thought in mind. Three months after we put the organization in place, the individual who took on the role of managing it approached me and admitted, "I now get what you mean about how transactions can be strategic." This new understanding came about more and more as each area learned how they were impacting the same customers— often at the same time, but with little to no knowledge of what the other functions were doing. The focus shifted from transactional silos to strategic problem-solving (i.e. asking how we could make the total customer experience a seamless one that consistently made issue resolution the primary principle). This allowed the team to begin to see endless opportunities to gain better knowledge of their customers as well as how their role played into the problem's solution. This resulted in better service, cost efficiency, and the elimination of process duplication. The solution was in elevating the service from a merely transactional approach to a solution-based strategy where the functions of the service center constantly worked behind the scenes to resolve the problem. The strategic perspective redefined how our transactional deliverables would not only work better, but work together to achieve great success.

HR leaders must be constantly thinking about the needs of the company. Today's new, strategic leadership must be the voice of capacity in the organization, understanding how to strategically manage and provide resources to meet the capacity needs of the organization both in the short and long term.

Why do CEOs need to invest in a strong internal HR consultant practice?

As I've pointed out, and will address further in the coming chapters, HR suffers from a bit of a bad rap. It has many different responsibilities when it comes to operational and tactical people processes, so it's not wrong to say that it doesn't, in fact, play a vital role in the processing and delivery of people-related processes. But, the mistake many CEOs make is in dismissing HR's potential. They seem only to understand it in terms of its nuts-and-bolts functions, without giving due respect to the higher level contributions it can make.

The value of investing in a strong HR practice that cultivates effective leaders cannot be overstated. Without a strong HR function, companies can expect to suffer from the following maladies:

1. **Impeded Corporate Growth (both organic and acquisition):** If HR is only involved at the later stages of the process, the department misses the opportunity to help shape the organizational model. Instead, corporate structure, cultural alignment, leadership capacity, and corporate culture get pigeon-holed,

becoming an afterthought after compliance and service delivery responsibilities are fulfilled. As a result, HR remains restricted in its ability to shape the culture for which it will inevitably be held responsible, which leads to delays and plenty of misunderstandings when they are charged with managing it. Consider how often mergers are unsuccessful. This usually stems from a lack of integration planning and cultural fit that gets handed to HR as an afterthought and not as an integral component to the success of the newly merged companies. Equally, lack of leadership talent to fulfill growth targets often falls squarely at HR's feet, and yet how often is HR proactively engaged in the strategy discussions that are deciding what markets to be in and what type of leaders are needed?

2. **Poorly Functioning Talent Acquisition Model:** If HR's focus remains on the process and tools of recruiting ("I need a person") versus its role as the connector to overall strategy ("We're planning on expanding into a new market; what resources will that take?"), the results can be delayed, or worse, and the end result could be missed market opportunities. At a high level, the decision to hire such key roles as C-suite managers should involve a top-level Talent Acquisition strategy. If HR works with the divisions of the company, a pool of resources will be identified in advance of need. If the function remains behind the pace of the company and without access to higher-level strategy meetings, it's just reacting with no context or insight.

3. **Crippled Compensation and Performance Reward Strategies:** If HR is not involved in the planning process, they're merely the administrator of programs and practices, not the innovator of new models and pay plans that could stimulate production and retention. The cost and expense of bringing in outside consultants can be avoided if you defer to the consultants you have right under your own roof. Your HR department should act as your internal consulting practice on

such matters, thinking out of the box for solutions to help you maintain, grow, and motivate your workforce.

4. **Top-Heavy Technology:** Confining HR to the production and delivery of dashboards of data with no context leads to missed opportunities to use technology appropriately and effectively. Performance assessment tools and HR technology produce people-related data, but without someone to translate it, the information alone does not automatically tell you how to use the data to expand and improve performance. Data for data's sake results in a heavy load of numbers without any explanation of what it really means, which can lead to a lot of misdirected decisions that could easily have been prevented.

5. **Delayed Customer Delivery:** HR most certainly considers the people resources of the company as its direct customers, but they also have an immediate impact on your external customers. Everything HR touches can have a positive or negative impact on day-to-day and long-term operations. An expertly run HR department that sits at the decision-making table can deliver a cohesive, agile, corporate culture that is able to meet the needs of the customer at every turn. An HR function that operates only in reaction mode adds little to no value, and is unable to help with the things that impact the customer...until it's too late.

As you can see, underestimating Human Resources only holds us back. This needs to change.

The state of a company without an elevated twenty-first-century HR team

Let's further discuss the dangers of operating a company without a strategic, highly performing, twenty-first century HR team.

While HR itself cannot sink a business on its own, it can find itself trapped into serving only as the provider of functional expertise, never being asked to contribute beyond the administrative level. The downside of operating only in the functional zone is a dearth of opportunities to proactively plan for strategic needs, expected or unexpected.

Reality HR, Season 3: Getting Immersed in the Acquisition Process

The Business Development teams at a company where I previously worked were focused on identifying new projects, which in this case meant the opportunity to build new power plants and acquire others for strategic positioning. With HR brought in only when it came time to handle process-driven deliverables (implementing compensation for business development people, and placing leaders to run the new projects), it was a challenge to show the value that HR could add during the *whole* business development cycle. HR was generally involved in the latter stages when many of the decisions had already been made. By then it was a question of playing catch-up: the assignment of who should be running the projects, what people would be needed to accomplish the goals, how to build the team to make the new unit successful, etc.

While all those details were important, it would have been far better to have gotten HR involved up front with the project's inception. Early involvement would have allowed HR to play an active role in determining the kind of talent needed to execute the project. We also could have raised questions that might have abated massive risk. For example, we could have asked about international employment issues, international talent search needs, and then been in a position to estimate the cost to build the capacity to get the best possible result out of the acquired plants or new plants. We could have asked if we had local relationships that could potentially elevate our marketing strategy—and so on. In the case of acquisitions, we could have helped execute on Day One by being closely integrated with Investor Relations, Communications, and the leadership team to present ourselves as a holistic company, not separate, uncoordinated departments. The easy option would have been to accept only being involved in the latter stages of Business Development; however, that is not how I nor the team viewed our role, and we were able to elevate our role and position.

While HR manages some of the greatest legal risks for the company and reviews policies regularly, it can play at a higher level. When HR plays solely in the governance role, it becomes an administrative, rule-driven entity that in today's world, is quite antiquated. CEOs need HR to ensure that governance is strong, but must also make sure it is equipped with the knowledge to enable flexibility and adaptability to deal with changing situations. As an example, if you have a salary structure in place and want to hire someone at a salary level outside that structure, you become an albatross around the neck of the organization if you simply state that the policy won't allow it. That's not what leaders want or need to hear when they need to make a vital hire. They know that keeping the governance structure in place is important, but what solutions are available to attract the talent needed? This requires HR to be creative and flexible with their solutions so that bureaucracy does not stifle agility. This isn't easy, but it most certainly can be done. When restricted to a rule-based, police-force role, HR becomes unbending, uncompromising, and unwilling to change its practices or viewpoints. It can snuff out the company's expansion.

If you believe as I do that HR's place in the organization— and the perception of that place—needs to be reevaluated, then you have to realize that such a transformation begins with you, the HR leader, as well as with the evolution of how we view HR's function. You must believe in the power of business-centric HR, and in the ability to run HR as a corporate entity in and of itself. This mindset requires you to assume the role of CEO of HR.

In business it's said, "You do the job to get the job." As you assemble your tool kit from the tools explained in this book—and when you show what you can do and deliver positive results—you'll begin to change the game and thereby the respectability of HR.

Run HR like a business, and it will succeed like any Fortune 500 company.

However, running a division isn't just about initiative— it's about opportunity. Leaders don't wait to be told to do something. They see an opening and they take it. Your ability to do this will set you apart as a strong HR partner.

Many of us judge our influence by our job titles and level of authority, but effective leadership is greater than the official title.

It means real respect, influence, and authority. Strong HR partners are confident, candid, and as a good friend once said to me, "[They're] willing to lose their job every day." Theirs is an independent voice that CEOs can rely on. They don't wait to be asked: they create opportunities to demonstrate impact and value. They're consulted on company issues, not just people concerns. They're respected for their intellect, their impeccable discretion, and their ability to grasp quickly where and how to add value.

Their many audiences see their efficacy at every turn:

» The board of directors engages them at multiple turns. They're seen as a trusted advisor, a conduit between the board and the senior executive team. They solicit board concerns, pairing mentoring and coaching opportunities between board and C-suite to expand the potential of everyone on the team. A valued HR partner is actively engaged in the conversations regarding board priorities, where the dialogue is beyond merely the people equation.

» CEOs don't see a "Yes" person, but a trusted confidant who can listen, provide thoughtful insight and independent counsel, and act as the CEO in their absence. CEOs and their HR partners seek to acquire the knowledge and skills that make for strong leadership, arming CEOs with the resources and abilities they need to be better leaders. Such HR professionals act as a bridge, a strategic alliance builder across the organization for the CEO. They're an invaluable part of any decision—nothing important happens without their counsel.

» C-suite management views the strong HR partner as a trusted advisor, a conduit, and coach who can assist CEOs in their own personal growth as well as provide perspective and insight. CEOs actively engage this power partner in discussions about their organizations, their people, and how to achieve maximum effectiveness.

» Middle management/line and staff-level see much more than its administrative capability. They recognize HR as a critical voice, a key organizational decision maker, and a trusted partner to help them navigate the corporate culture and plan their futures effectively.

Smart, successful leaders realize that their success, or lack thereof, depends largely on their ability to capitalize on opportunities. The top HR performers I envision think like sole proprietors. They don't wait for directions: they seize opportunities. They know their very survival depends on this speed and agility. Strategic, business-centric HR leaders focus on increasing profitability and value for all stakeholders. They view the company—and their role within it—through a larger lens. They define the "how" and source the "who." For every opportunity—from mergers and acquisitions to global expansion and managing the global brand—HR leaders see how to make it a reality and who to tap to help the company get there.

This is the foundation for making HR the career you really want, and will be the focus of our work together in this book. Your mission, should you choose to accept it, is to expand your vision and scope and become this new strategic, business- centric HR leader.

And, your new job title is Chief Capacity Officer.

Reality HR, Season 4: Seizing the Moment

One of my greatest challenges was the creation and rollout of a global compensation program—within a six-month window. The implementation was a make-or-break decision for the company with incredibly high stakes: the potential to save over a million dollars, and that was just in Corporate Headquarters expenses. But, we had a hard sell on our hands; it meant dismantling a culture of individual decision makers and replacing it with a structured process, guidelines, and discipline for all compensation decisions.

Such a rollout wouldn't have been possible without our COO and CEO buying in. But even with that significant support, we received considerable pushback from other leadership, claiming the new compensation program was taking away their rights to make key decisions when it came to the compensation of their talent. There were accusations that HR was trying to be "all-powerful." In other words, we were to remain a service provider, not part of the decision-making process.

The implementation resulted in a huge shift, and I can't say that it was a perfect process. The execution of the new plan unearthed a lot of baggage within the business, resulting in many discussions with the executive team about implementing it. We addressed every possible concern: could it lead to increased costs, would HR become the ultimate decision makers and not the business, would it make our company a bureaucratic, paper-and-policy-driven nightmare?

We weathered the storm like professionals. When it comes to change management, you have to go in with the understanding that it will cause disruption and that many won't like it. We were able to show that their concerns were unfounded; HR wasn't running things, but rather attempting to help things run more smoothly. The bottom line is that some people loved it and others hated it. But, there was no denying that the new system drove efficiency and transparency. As opposed to it becoming a bureaucratic, HR-driven program, it actually made the compensation system easier to manage and understand. Many employees suddenly had a much clearer view of their performance, and the business had a standardized, decision-making process around compensation.

Sure, I would have loved to have twelve months to build a robust, change management plan and roll things out in a more methodical manner. The reality is that you have to make a judgment call. Do you seize the opportunity to implement a solution you know is right for the company, realizing at the same time that you're pushing against the inertia of those who think decision-making in this area is something of an inalienable right for them? Or, do you sit on your hands because you're afraid to ruffle feathers? I think I would make the same decision again.

We learned throughout the process via multiple conversations with the management team that we needed to be open to continual refinement, and perhaps more importantly, that we should have engaged the skeptics earlier. My biggest lesson was that I needed to involve all stakeholders early on, and take dissent as an opportunity to make the dissenters part of the process. If they don't like it, let them come to the table with ideas about how to shape it. Involvement creates less room for criticism, and the input can create a stronger process owned by the very people who need to utilize it for the overall success of the company.

Five Things to Remember

1 The business environment is more complex and changing more rapidly than ever before.

2 It is crucial that the C-suite and senior management have key people at the decision-making table who can solve problems from an organization-wide, big-picture view.

3 Capacity-centric HR leaders must understand how to strategically manage resources to fit the capacity needs of the organization.

4 The perception of HR's role within and outside an organization needs to change in order for HR to achieve its business-centric focus, and exponentially increase its value to the organization.

5 Business-centric HR leaders are their organizations' Chief Capacity Officers.

2

BEHIND THE SCENES NO MORE

The Enormous Untapped Potential of HR

Perhaps the time has come to say it out loud: we must be focused and purposeful in how we, as HR professionals, act in the workplace and talk about our profession, reflecting what HR really can do.

The challenges that face HR today

I get it. You get it: *we're busy.*

We're so busy, in fact, that we're bogged down in a considerable number of challenges. Let's look at what we're up against in the modern organization.

HR has the broadest range of responsibilities of any executive field

In the modern organization, HR is involved in almost every aspect at some level. HR supports every department from Manufacturing to Marketing, from Finance to Operations. In many cases, its involvement is not very deep; but the accountability for the success of the parts we own, as well as for those we don't directly own, is incredibly high.

Talent acquisition is under our jurisdiction, and it's intensely complicated. It's not about charts and meetings and succession plans; it's about understanding the depth of the talent pool and developing innovative ways to attract and develop the best.

During my tenure at AES, like many companies hit by the financial crisis, we needed to make some strategic decisions to reduce costs and realign our business model for a period of slow growth. Our new operating model required us to have a lean, but high-performing business development team, with a separate operations team, focused on driving performance in our existing market presences.

The requirement to significantly reduce the number of business development people could have been done in many different ways: each leader could have been told to cut x-number of heads, specific groups might have been eliminated, we could have made cuts based on the number of deals people had closed, or any combination of the above.

The reality was that this was not simply a head count reduction decision; it was critical that we made decisions that protected our ability to ramp up business development when the market conditions improved. Relationships with key stakeholders take time to nurture; getting to grips with and understanding the complexity of the market, understanding how to put together an appropriate financial model all factored in the decision making process. Simply put, these capabilities were not something that an individual could learn in a matter of days.

The decision around who to keep and who to let go was based on what would be best for the company in the longer term.

We took a strategic view, assessing all the people using a thorough and robust process, discounting where they were located in the world and what they did, and vetting them through an exhaustive assessment process. We carefully evaluated what type of people would be needed to meet our revised strategy, which led us to conclusions different from those we would have reached had we gone the typical head count route, or simply assumed that they were not located in the right country. My point is that head count reduction takes on many guises, and it is important to understand that to be effective. You have to start by understanding the strategic implications of your actions, and not simply focus on the tactical aspects of cost reduction. Doing so means that you are making business decisions, not simply carrying out an HR activity.

HR also has had a major role to play in the area of compensation, and this has become increasingly important for publicly-traded companies in the U.S., where greater shareholder scrutiny and SEC regulations have raised the visibility around executive compensation. HR's role is not simply to administer the rules and regulations, but to strategically advise and design programs that meet the objectives of the company and its stakeholders. Our role becomes one of interpreter, bridging the languages of compliance and corporate strategy, so the goals of the company are achieved both within the guidelines of the government as well as the objectives set forth by the overall corporate plan.

HR is also expected to provide both strategic direction and administrative expertise when it comes to benefits and payroll. While many would place these functions firmly in the administrative camp, I beg to differ. Finding ways to think outside the box when it comes to pay-program development and design can elevate these typical "back-office" functions to be viewed as vitally important factors of success that build value and HR credibility.

In my opinion, the most underutilized and often neglected function within HR today is organizational. I liken HR's role in this area to what CEOs do when they formulate the overall company performance plan and strategy. HR's role as advisor is important and few play it well, leaving the majority of organizational design work in the hands of consultants or other divisional leaders. Executed effectively, however, this role is vital in creating the best possible organizational structure by leading and facilitating discussions, and then helping the organization find solutions that best fit its needs. It is yet another example of a business line that HR has to reconsider in its efforts to assert its authority over its own domain, that of capacity ownership.

In many companies, HR winds up with high-stakes responsibility without any real authority

HR tends to be a support function in many organizations, a behind-the-scenes player. People and organization decisions have a major impact on a company, and yet we don't generally control a large part of the company's destiny in these areas. We have yet to be thought of as a major part of the corporation.

Stop for a moment and think about this. Consider all the verticals/lines/products/processes within a company. It begs the question of whether we can be effective in our delivery across all these departments. The sheer complexity of having to manage such a broad set of responsibilities makes it difficult to be expert in all of them. By continuing to think of HR as a service function, we miss the opportunity to see in what way we might be most effective. Then, too, we perhaps have a tendency to be too broad and overextend ourselves.

It's not surprising that many of the HR transformations of the past ten to fifteen years have focused on consolidating functional expertise and outsourcing. Our transformation has been more static, and without a vision of what a redefining of our verticals would look like. The challenge for us is to look at our functional areas and make robust strategic choices about what to focus on—in what areas we can truly provide value differentiation—and then hire and develop the right talent to make it happen.

The state of companies with task-focused HR silos

As a result of having a great deal of the HR department's control of its workload out of the hands of HR managers, many of these managers, not unexpectedly, tend to focus on those things that they can, in fact, control and manage: the traditional administrative duties. The expanded role, the advisory positions, the digging deeper into the other departments they support to ask questions like, "Why are we doing things this way?"—these matters are left for another day, sometime in the future. Right now, they're in the weeds.

Interestingly, a comparison of HR today and twenty years ago shows that the discipline hasn't moved away much from its perennial complaints. The discipline seems to be stuck in a circle of administrative tasks, essentially running in place. And even when HR takes on one of its most important tasks—identifying and acquiring talent for the organization—it tends to do so as an end in and of itself. For example, "We need five bodies in sales" is seen as the only goal rather than as the means to reach a bigger goal— which requires us to think more deeply as we ask, "How do we find the best people to increase sales by 25 percent this year?"

"We need five bodies in sales," gives no reason for those "bodies" to be anything other than warm and mostly breathing. It's simply a task, and recruiting will likely go find mostly inadequate people for those positions, leaving the division no better off than it was originally. There is no context, no higher reason given to help the recruiter find the right people to achieve that 25 percent sales increase goal. Recruiting the right people to achieve that level of growth is a very important strategic initiative. Its success or failure affects everyone else in the company. This is just one of many reasons why HR must be in a position to put company goals and performance ahead of merely completing processing tasks.

Periodically, self-styled gurus and consultants will put forth a "new model" for HR. I have seen and implemented many of these over my career. Each revolutionary program promises change for everyone. However, my experience is that it usually does not happen. Why? Because regardless of how sexy the new model is, if the HR professionals don't buy into it and believe in it, it's not going to happen.

In my experience, new models don't reorient the HR profession. HR practitioners do.

We are the problem as well as the solution!

It's time for us, as HR professionals, to stare into the mirror and take a hard look at ourselves. As much as we want HR to be a strategic partner in our organizations and have the ever-elusive seat at the C-suite table, the reality is that we are not perceived as that strategic partner. In fact, this perception may well be valid and even somewhat justified from the standpoint not only of CEOs and corporate leaders, or from students, but also from young professionals already in HR.

These talented young HR professionals, early in their careers, have the vision and desire to get into the real work of HR that we've discussed here. They are seeking the mentorship and guidance that will help them live up to their potential in the organization. But, to their disappointment, many of them discover what appears to be a vacuum both in opportunities for career development and in strong role models to help them get there.

We, as professionals, have not been aggressive enough in working toward changing the shape, form, and substance of HR; we have not worked hard enough to pass that sense of urgency on to those around us. We need to change this. We see the enormous potential HR has to be an agent of positive change in our organizations. So, let's act on this knowledge; let it be reflected in the way we talk about our profession, and show what HR can really do.

Could HR have saved them?

The collapse of companies like Lehman Brothers, the WorldCom crisis, and even Toyota's recall of over nine million cars highlight some of the many missed opportunities for HR to have stepped up and shifted into a capacity-driven role. In each of these examples, there were some recurring themes. A lack of checks and balances, along with a failure to "call out" practices many knew were not correct, led to the destruction of some or all of these companies. Unchallenged, poor leadership behaviors allowed a culture filled with bad ideas to fester.

Could HR have saved these companies? Honestly, I don't know. What I do know is that there were likely occasions where HR leaders could have stepped in, when their voices should have been loud and clear, and they should have been having conversations with the board about their concerns and insights. I mentioned earlier that a great friend and highly-accomplished HR executive told me the best advice he'd ever received about what it takes to be a top CHRO is to be prepared to lose your job every day. That means being willing to be the lone voice of reason when nothing seems reasonable, even when you know that, despite your best efforts, you alone cannot turn the ship around. Having the courage to know that you need to solicit help despite what it may mean for you personally is when you demonstrate "organizational ego" and not "individual ego." That action alone can be what saves companies from falling into the same trap as the above-mentioned companies, which was allowing some people with highly questionable motives along with bad leadership practices to stay in place even when they knew it was wrong. Someone somewhere knew this would happen.

The future of the workplace

Pick up any article or research paper—from McKinsey's "War for Talent" (2000) to the most recent Deloitte study to the "Conference Board CEO Challenge 2014" report—and the message is clear: our workplace is rapidly changing. A recent PricewaterhouseCoopers report points out that two-thirds of the CEOs in their Annual Global CEO survey believe that HR is not well prepared to address the challenges facing it today, whether in the areas of technology, government regulations, market opportunity, or cost.

They all point to the pace of change, the need to alter operational models and adapt them to today's corporate environment. This includes the central importance of being agile and willing to adapt.

I truly believe that if HR ever needed an opportunity to demonstrate what it can do, that opportunity has arrived. We could not have been presented with a better set of circumstances to show what we can do. Taking on the mantle of Chief Capacity Officer means being at the center of these transformative changes by remaining an active leader, not a reactive one.

There are several ways to accomplish this:

» Don't wait to get into the organizational structure conversation—be a change generator, not a change implementer.

» The Digital Age is not new, but the impact of its evolution is taking on a different meaning for companies today. Social Media Analytics and cloud technology are not only changing how companies interact with customers, but also how they organize and structure their own organization to deliver results.

» A significant gap that we need to close is how to not only engage, but also lead the discussion about the organizational operating model.

We can do this by asking ourselves these questions:

Can you effectively engage and lead a discussion on how different operating structures impact cost? Or, how the organizational structure fits and aligns to the markets and customers your company serves? How does that same structure meet governance and regulation requirements? How does it facilitate the replication and transfer knowledge of it?

If you cannot, then you are not in a position to be an influential voice in discussions about strategy and organizational design. *Will you do what it takes to change your position in the company?*

If you are not yet in this position, but you want to be, you need to become versed in the value and impact of designing a new operating model. *Will you change direction to achieve a higher level of influence?*

Today's CEOs are focused on things like innovation, new technologies, regulation, and social outcomes. We need to be focused on them, too. If we are not, if we are not helping our CEOs meet today's business challenges in these crucial areas, then we are not builders of capacity. We are not in charge of our destiny.

It starts with the right organizational model

The workplace of today and tomorrow is not centered on a building or a place where people go to work; it is likely to be more fluid and flexible. This is not anything endemic to the organizational model; technology has been changing how we do business for several decades. The role of Chief Capacity Officer means driving the discussion about the right organizational model for the company and how it impacts the overall culture, and management structure, and whether the people-related processes we espouse are necessary for moving the company forward. We must become proactive partners in these discussions to add value and gain ground with our leadership team.

HR needs to anticipate how to transform the talent debate

We have spent decades, it seems, disappointing CEOs when it comes to delivering on talent. CEOs continue to cite talent as being one of their top challenges and yet HR does not appear to be delivering. The number of CEO changes that happen – average tenure for CEO is 3-5 years, which begs the question: are we doing sufficient due diligence when it comes to appointments at this level? If 2 out of 3 times, the organization has to seek to fill a position by going outside versus filling it from someone in the talent pipeline or succession chart, we have to ask ourselves what's not working – and reevaluate whether our processes are truly outcome driven versus just being output driven. Although we surely need to look in the mirror, we should not necessarily beat ourselves up and say we were wrong, or we didn't do it right. Instead, we should simply recognize that we need to change how we go about recruiting and cultivating talent. Just like technology is transforming how we live, work, and play, and the winners in this field are not following convention, perhaps the time for us has come to not follow convention when it comes to talent and talent practices.

I give some ideas on how to do this later in the book, but it starts with being willing to go back and really ask whether all our investments in competency models and performance planning tools have yielded the value we hoped they would. Perhaps they're overused or have taken on a life of their own, but they're not contributing to the overall mission. I am not arguing for them to be dismissed completely, but maybe we should be asking ourselves tough questions about what competencies we should be focused on. The one-size-fits-all strategy does not necessarily align with a company strategy. If a company has divisions that are in different stages of the business lifecycle, they need different skills to lead them to success. Yet we tend to treat them all the same.

There is a solution

If I step back a little further and look objectively at development programs targeted for our profession, I feel like I want to shout, "Stop!"

Let's not teach our teams about HR from just a functional perspective; let's expand our capabilities.

We need to teach the definition of a strategy, build a divisional and corporate performance plan, and how to deliver on those objectives. Let's talk about shareholders and stakeholders in meaningful ways that connect them to the work of our group; let's expand knowledge about our relationship to the company.

The HR makeover we want and need starts with each of us! Let's not just say we are transforming, reengineering or redesigning HR. Instead, let's do something about it before CEOs and stakeholders decide to rely even more on consultants and outside resources to provide the business-centric value we can already bring. Let's make sure the processes of HR excite and engage our constituents. Let's show them how it's really possible for HR to change the game.

We do not need to live by the old-guard paradigm and definitions.

Leaders see the way forward. So let's lead.

Five Things to Remember

1 The perception of our role in HR is bound up with administrative and functional duty. It persists because we allow it.

2 Although we are saddled with a tremendous number of tasks and responsibilities, if we evolve to a more strategic mindset, these can become our opportunities to change the game for ourselves. We have the opportunity to speak on our behalf, to advocate for and demonstrate the true potential for our role in our organizations.

3 The tools with which we perform our duties will become our greatest assets as long as we can begin to think of them in terms of building capacity.

4 Function delivers the strategy, and it is in strategic thinking that our new future as leaders awaits us.

5 Leaders shape the vision of the organization, so start thinking like a visionary.

3
BEYOND MODELS
The Capacity-Centric Mindset

It's not the model; it's the mindset

HR can be a vital, strategic, and defining force in an organization. Done right, HR doesn't need a seat at the table because it *is* the table: the place where things are considered, made possible, and executed.

The job of HR can be as cool as you want it to be. It depends on what type of approach you have toward the job. Come at it from a stakeholder-driven point of view, and you can get into every aspect of an organization. You can challenge yourself to think beyond your experience, look for new ways to do things and have a real impact.

I do not know many jobs that can have as wide an impact as HR. Over the years, there is not one functional area of an organization that I have not touched in some way, especially when I have looked at it from the viewpoint of the C-suite. The difference between being function centric and capacity centric changes both your start and end point.

Let's look at helping an organization realize a new strategic vision. When we start looking at executing the strategy, the big picture can get lost in the details. What makes HR really significant is when you can bring that big picture back to the table and discover the disconnection between the company's objectives and its challenges around capacity—because capacity is the way they'll achieve those goals, every single time.

It doesn't so much matter how you design the organization model largely because it's about talent needed to execute it. If you don't understand the skills and capabilities needed, it does not matter if you have the best organizational design; you don't have the skills to deliver what's needed. It's like building a house on a shaky foundation—it won't remain standing. The HR issue has never been about functional expertise. We have many people who have that in spades. Our issue is going beyond the comfort zone of functional expertise and playing at a higher level.

Shifting the focus: function vs. consultancy

The subtitle above completely and simply lays out the core of what capacity-centric HR means to me. Traditional HR has always been the reliable function—every day, doing its administrative duties, very task-oriented—but never with a seat at the decision-making table, never really stretching to reach its full potential. Here are a few examples that further illustrate that distinction:

At Honeywell, our acquisitions required us to often integrate companies with very different cultures. For example, one acquisition involved an entrepreneurial, product-based company making fire alarms that we combined with a business which had a highly process driven culture. The issue with integrating these two cultures was defining the right model that would keep a high level of quality and process discipline while remaining quick to market. The parent corporation was simultaneously seeking to reduce costs in order to remain market competitive. In a product-focused market, the risk is always that your product is a commodity play, that there are numerous other companies who can provide the same product at a much lower cost. Competing in this type of market requires a very lean manufacturing and sales structure in order to leverage overall margins. We also had a new president from a very fast-moving, new-product-turnaround culture coming in to oversee the new structure. In viewing his new portfolio, he quickly pointed out that we were too slow to react. Over time, lengthy processes and process reviews along with top-heavy, overly-bureaucratic organizational structures had resulted in unnecessary people and operational costs, which hampered the ability to react quickly to market conditions.

This is when I got to learn about the power of HR as a strategic partner. My manager was in the middle of all the discussions, proving to be a strong asset who had the full trust and support of management earned through his understanding of what made their divisions run. This ranged from the impact of certain sales models on product margin, to why organizational structures with six levels of leadership not only added cost, but duplication and inefficiency, to the impact of location and what it did to the cost model. The discussions were numerous, as were the decisions that needed to be made: what would happen if we set up manufacturing in a low-cost country? Would that be possible? Would the talent capacity be there? How would we attract and develop that talent? What change in management plan would we need to ensure that we created efficiency without losing market share or quality?

We ended up reducing millions of dollars of costs. HR was critical to this change effort because it started from a company-first perspective.

Anticipation trumps reaction...every time

Being a change-generator in your organization, and establishing HR itself as a change generator means that you will have to stand up and advocate for change when required. There have been many times in my career where I have taken advantage of the opportunity to embrace and generate change in a particular role or organization. Here are some examples:

Reality HR, Season 5: Ditching the Talent 9 Block Assessment Tool

One of the best talent evaluation discussions I've ever engaged in followed a spirited discussion with the CEO, who was eager to find a way to reduce the amount of executive time spent on the talent process. We debated for a long time before I realized that some of his points were valid. We were, in reality, not getting everything we could or should be getting from the process. So, we redesigned the process. We cut a two-day process down to one day, and discarded the usual tools for discussing the top eighty people in the company. We designed a completely new process; we removed previous assessment data (talent ratings, etc.) and simply showed picture cards.

We removed titles and individual rankings from the discussion, and simply showed picture cards of each person. We then asked people to decide whether the person—based on capabilities and performance—was an "up" (someone with potential to go much further in the organization), a "blocker" (a consistent underperfomer who might also occupy a key position that should be held by an "up", or a "keep" (a solid performer). By focusing our discussion solely on the contrast in votes, we were able to decide objectively which roles were pivotal and which people were key. The result was more strategic decision-making in less time, and a lasting change to the company's practice of talent reviews that executives now look forward to participating in.

We ended up making tough people decisions, resulting in letting lower performers go, increasing and raising the bar for those who were considered high potential, and placing more rigor around our hiring/placement decisions for key roles. We coupled that with evaluating compensation decisions to review whether we were consistent in how we were awarding our performers and talent. In some cases, we discovered glaring inconsistencies in how we evaluated talent and the resulting pay decisions. It made the talent/performance conversation richer, and drove better performance and pay decisions that were linked to both individual and company performance.

AES is a global company, and a critical factor for sustained growth was the development of its markets by the rotation of talented executives who would take assignments for a period of time to help develop those markets around the world. Unlike many companies with typical ex-pat programs that are large enough to be able to absorb the cost of sending people on two-year assignments and then have them return to their home country, we found ourselves in a situation where (1) our divisions were not of a size where they could necessarily support that kind of program; (2) many of our ex-pats were non-US nationals who, once they left their home country, lost all Social Security, pension rights, and employment continuation; and (3) the design of a standard expatriate program did not align with our needs. Our challenge was to come up with a solution whereby talented people would be attracted to take on these leadership positions, knowing that their next move would be. At the same time, we needed to keep their compensation attractive, and prevent them from losing entitlements they would have if they stayed in their current role.

This required the definition of a whole new compensation structure, which included new thinking around the problem of pensions. The eventual solution was conceived in tandem with

PricewaterhouseCoopers, who was willing to help push the envelope from a design perspective to come up with a new way to address the need for a global expatriate program. This meant striking out on our own to create and implement such a program, plus we had to show the return on investment for the company. Our solution ended up lowering overall costs since we avoided large, buy-out expenses for lost benefits, and increased the talent pool attracted to take on these global ex-pat roles. It also led to a more consistent approach to managing talent at a company-wide level.

Don't fall back into your comfort zone

Because so many HR professionals believe that organizations need HR for the basics of administration, it's easy to retreat into this functionalism because it is a comfort zone—structure, discipline, and job security.

I am here to tell you that if you really want to excel and thrive in HR, if you want to be a true leader in HR, you must change your comfort zone. The future of HR in modern organizations will continue to evolve beyond the administrative function. What shape HR will ultimately take is unclear, but the one thing that is certain is that, like the organizations of which it is a part, change will be the rule, not the exception.

Find simple, effective ways to do things differently. Add value with your creativity. Make change your friend.

HR is an open ticket to explore

To explore is to embrace the unknown, to do something you've never done before. When most of us think of the word "explore," we conjure up images from a National Geographic documentary. But, the same spirit of adventure and excitement can be brought to how we approach our work.

The best entrepreneurs are consummate explorers. They are constantly looking at new ideas and new markets, and confronting new challenges. There is no reason I can think of why an HR professional should not operate from exactly that same mindset. You can't buy a company, move a factory, merge with another company, sell a division, open a location, or bring out a new product line without embracing the unknown, and thinking about resources and capacity. Those challenges and opportunities should be the new frontier for HR. However, you won't get there if you fall back into the administrative comfort zone. You must be willing to take a stand. Generally speaking, in most organizations, there are not many people willing to do that. Being a leader in the new world of HR means you must be the one to stand up and speak and ask the tough questions that are relevant, or even critical to the success of your organization.

HR is truly an open ticket to explore the peaks and valleys of the corporate world. It's a unique position of opportunity that can have tremendous value to any organization, and be incredibly fulfilling personally, as well.

If you want to be the CEO of HR in your organization, your thinking must go beyond the current state of the art. Traditional HR has focused on activities that are function centric; the new HR must be business centric.

And, as the owner of HR, this is what must guide your decision-making process as well.

Strategic HR leaders think like business owners. They focus on increasing the profitability and value for all stakeholders. Viewing the company through a wider lens is the foundation for making the shift to your role as a top-performing HR professional.

Your new doctrine is "performance first."

"Performance First" Doctrine

Ask:
"What will it really take?"
for every task under your purview, and account for every factor.

It's the difference between spending a budget and building one.

It's the difference between being a general contractor and being an architect.

As I said before, our new role is to define the "how" and find the right "who" for every opportunity—from mergers and acquisitions to global expansion to managing the global brand.

OK, now you "own" HR. What does that mean?

With this shift in thinking comes a shift in how you attack just about every problem or challenge that you face. It's this shift in thinking that puts you in a position to be your organization's Chief Capacity Officer.

And, your tool to winning in this new role is The Capacity Framework, which we will look at in detail in the next chapter.

Five Things to Remember

1 HR can be a vital, strategic, and defining force in an organization.

2 Be involved in the larger aspects of running the company versus focusing solely on your processes.

3 We have to make sure we are not doing HR for HR's sake. For every initiative, system, tool, or process we propose, we need to constantly be asking ourselves "why are we doing this? Is it adding value to the company?"

4 Don't fall back into your comfort zone.

5 HR is an open ticket to explore the larger corporate world.

4

THE CAPACITY FRAMEWORK

The Ultimate Tool for Positive Transformation

H R can be a discipline of creative design. It's creative, not reactive. It's not just about the application of models. It's about constantly evolving those models. Other than the CEO and COO, perhaps, no one else in the organization has the same opportunity that you do. HR touches all aspects of the company. If you have the strategic and creative vision, you have a better view of what needs to be done to succeed than just about anyone else.

The Capacity Framework

Strategic HR leaders must think like corporate owners, focusing on increasing the profitability and value for all stakeholders. Viewing the company from this more encompassing perspective is the foundation for making the shift to an elevated role as a top HR professional.

What we've yet to address are the tools through which assessment, understanding, and ultimately change in the organization can occur. What's needed is a way to make decisions in regard to capacity—a decision-making framework, if you will. This is where we will introduce the right tool for the job, the cornerstone of the Chief Capacity Officer's practice: the Capacity Framework. Before we go into the tool itself, we should talk about the proper mindset of the person using it. Viewing the company through an elevated, business centric lens will allow for a higher level of vision and understanding on the part of the decision-maker. This is key to using an elevated framework like the one I'm about to introduce. So, let's talk about the capacity of the mind of the decision makers, or their capacity to view the company.

We've talked about the similarities of a top-performing CEO and that of his CHRO compatriot. If you look at companies that lack vision, bravado, and foresight worldwide, you'll see that there are similarities right down the line. Looking at the four dimensions below, the gap between high and low performing companies is clear.

Capacity Framework for the CEO

◐ LOW CAPACITY

VISION	STRATEGY	SOLUTIONS	LEADERSHIP BRAND
Rooted solely in the next move	How do we make the next move	Product bias; lack of vision	Lack of talented leadership

◐ MID-LEVEL CAPACITY

VISION	STRATEGY	SOLUTIONS	LEADERSHIP BRAND
Reacting to what the next move should be	Routine, cyclical strategy refreshes	Products and services	Good leaders present, but lack breadth and/or depth

● HIGH CAPACITY

VISION	STRATEGY	SOLUTIONS	LEADERSHIP BRAND
Seeing the ultimate success model and market position	Creating a path to prominence: who, what, when, where and why	Corporate impact bias	Talented, credible leadership that mobilizes the entire organization

Note the overall themes here:

Low-capacity leadership lives in the present, barely able to look up from today's problems to solve tomorrow's. They have a stair-stepper mentality, putting out fires, and looking for quick solutions to cash flow or other issues. They can barely see above their desks; they fight for position at every turn; they lack talented leadership that can deliver outside of set processes. Their corporations are usually fraught with power struggles, a lack of leadership respect, and no clear vision for anyone inside the company. Their shelf life may be longer than you think, but success on a grand scale will always remain outside their grasp.

Mid-level capacity leadership is where a lot of companies operate today. They're not constantly putting out fires, but they're reacting to what's happening rather than leading the charge for change. They look at their processes, and tinker with organizational and delivery models because they see others doing it. They have the sense to expand from just delivering products ("We make this") to products and services ("We make this AND we're also in the business of helping to deliver a service to support you and make your life easier with respect to that product."). They have good leadership, but it may not offer the wide variety of challenges that would keep the group stimulated. They may be disjointed in leadership, or key talent may be looking elsewhere for strong leadership passion.

High-capacity leadership is where companies simply shine with a CEO of real vision. It handles current issues by driving toward a vision of the future, a clear path to prominence, with a team filled with passion. They're flexible in the face of market conditions because they've seen the next steps, have an eye toward making the company agile by the use of future-thinking tools, and are not afraid to turn on a dime to realize their vision of where they desire to be. The leadership is talented and passionate, driven to success, and was gathered by a leader to whom they have entrusted their careers. They believe in that CEO's vision and in the person who has charged them to bring it to life.

Let's look at a framework for capacity for the CHRO in the same manner:

Capacity Framework for the CHRO/ Top HR Officer

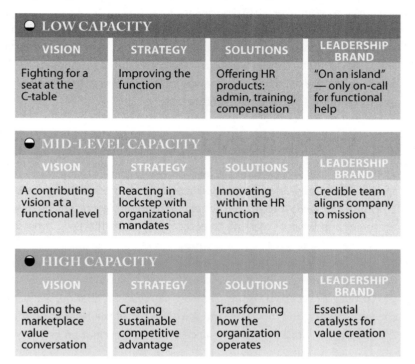

● LOW CAPACITY			
VISION	**STRATEGY**	**SOLUTIONS**	**LEADERSHIP BRAND**
Fighting for a seat at the C-table	Improving the function	Offering HR products: admin, training, compensation	"On an island" — only on-call for functional help

● MID-LEVEL CAPACITY			
VISION	**STRATEGY**	**SOLUTIONS**	**LEADERSHIP BRAND**
A contributing vision at a functional level	Reacting in lockstep with organizational mandates	Innovating within the HR function	Credible team aligns company to mission

● HIGH CAPACITY			
VISION	**STRATEGY**	**SOLUTIONS**	**LEADERSHIP BRAND**
Leading the marketplace value conversation	Creating sustainable competitive advantage	Transforming how the organization operates	Essential catalysts for value creation

Low-capacity HR leadership is essentially powerless outside of their official titles. They constantly fight for respect and a voice in corporate decisions, and are largely relegated to delivering solutions to issues resulting from choices made in their absence. They tinker with the HR function itself because it's the only thing over which they have any real authority. They offer basic HR tools to prove the worth of the department, but without a larger focus or the ability to translate the results into corporate language, they're mostly unused. They remain separate and apart from the real decision-making, "on call" to react to decisions that affect them with no ability to do anything but follow orders.

Mid-level capacity HR management is in a better place. They at least have some voice in what's happening, but no real ability to see beyond immediate concerns. They remain current with market tools, but with no real power to do anything outside the scope of the company's current course. These HR leaders provide higher-level innovation within the confines of the HR function because they're at least aligned with the company's initiatives. But their credibility continues to rely solely upon their ability to deliver on company directives. Strategic and outward-reaching, sadly, they are not.

High-capacity HR professionals, on the other hand, are in step with their visionary CEO counterparts. They consistently look for market intelligence to drive a vision for HR that matches or exceeds that of the CEO. They lead discussions about creating competitive advantage. They bring capacity into the talks at every turn, constantly seeking new resources and ways of working to accomplish great things not only in the here and now, but also in the bright, shining future. They lead with an eye toward corporate results, transforming the way the company operates, and shaping the discussion of how to best utilize resources so the company exceeds its goals. They are catalysts for change, well-respected leaders who innovate, and have the ear of the board and the C-suite, always with an eye on the prize of global domination.

Clearly, we would all love to shift over to the High-Capacity model as soon as possible. So let's talk a bit more about those four factors that drive the Capacity Framework, the tool through which all decisions regarding capacity are made.

The four dimensions of capacity-driven leadership

Vision

Vision is the ability to see opportunities, strategic advantages, new products, and the best positioning of the brand. It goes above mere planning: it involves foresight, a view of where the company and its markets are going, how it will get there, and what means will be used to get it there. Vision is creative but rooted in fact, bolstered by hard data that supports all decisions that must be made and all actions that must be taken to realize it. It's a high-level view of what the company can be, when accompanied by a strategic plan to bring it to fruition.

Key components:

Creative thinking, expansive knowledge, ability to see the business beyond your own deliverables and tasks, research, interpretation of information, understanding stakeholders.

How it impacts capacity:

Capacity cannot exist without a vision for its future. The ability to keep a future state in your mind's eye for where the corporation will go means planning for its capacity to reach that ideal place. Vision means constantly viewing what will need to be done to reach that place of top performance, always ensuring that where you're going is where you want to be.

How to use it effectively:

The creation of an overall vision for both HR and for the corporate entity is the crucial first step in any action planning. It's the beginning of setting the direction for capacity-driven business. It defines where you want to go and how you will get there. Set your vision and move toward it with vigor, but never hold it so dear that it can't be adjusted if your overall objectives change.

Your vision is the prize all eyes must be on, and as the captain of the ship, you must tell your crew where to go. The vision is the star you sail toward. Set your course accordingly, making any necessary adjustments as you go.

Success trajectory:

Your vision will need to be the same as your organization's or exceed it. Note the positions of HR described below, first, when it has less vision than the organization, and second, when it outperforms and leads the company according to its vision in the Capacity Framework. On which team would you rather be?

VISION

When the CEO perceptions surpass HR:

When the vision of the organization outstrips that of the HR department, HR is challenged to upgrade their team and/or completely rethink their organizational model and strategy without wholesale disruption to the firm.

In order to help HR in these efforts, the C-suite of the organization must make this a priority action item, demanding greater performance from the group. Excluding the HR team from developing or engaging in designing the Vision, or accepting subpar performance from them will only hurt the organization as a whole. The CEO must hold HR accountable for a new HR model that does not short circuit the enterprise.

When HR's perspective surpasses the CEO's

When HR's vision for its role and impact on the organization is greater than that of the organization, HR leads the change agenda with the CEO, executing strategic initiatives within the organization that lead it to greater profitability.

Organizations that possess such progressive HR groups should enroll them at every step. Relying on HR's Market Intelligence and Internal Communication's skills can help in aligning the organization around the vision.

Strategy

Strategy is the way we execute the vision that we've set for our- selves; it's the way we play the game—the moves we make, the projects and initiatives we will under-take, the decisions that will have to be made and executed. All of these individual components comprise a strategy. Without strategy, a vision is merely a lofty idea. Strategy is what brings it to life.

Key components:

Stakeholder involvement, market knowledge, resource management, budgetary accountability, process creation and management, project and time line management, deadline orientation, mental agility.

How it impacts capacity:

Strategy is the where, how, and what of the way in which capacity will be used to realize the vision. Strategy is a plan to create capacity where it doesn't currently exist, to utilize it to its fullest advantage where it thrives, and to cut losses and redeploy it when it makes sense to exit a less advantageous situation. All of these moves are strategic in nature, and are the lifeline of how capacity-driven businesses operates.

How to use it effectively:

Strategy is best conceived in relation to your stakeholders. It must be developed simultaneously with your C-suite team as well as your own team, constantly ensuring that the steps you wish to take are the right ones and that you have the tools you need to complete your journey. You should constantly be asking if your process is the right one, and hold it up to desired corporate results to ensure you're on target with cost, return on investment, and the carrying-out of the institution's overall performance plan. Strategy is where we come to make our vision a reality, and we won't be deterred until the game is won.

Success trajectory:

HR must always strive to understand and deliver on the strategic initiatives of its company, but it is possible to exceed those goals and set an even more exciting direction. Below is an example of an HR division that remains behind the strategic thinking of its shareholders, and another example of one that leads them. Note the differences between the two, and decide how you're going to motivate your team to realize your vision:

STRATEGY

When the CEO perceptions surpass HR:

When the strategy of the organization outstrips that of the HR function, the HR team will find itself relegated to a transactional role, preoccupied by improving their function. The #1 action HR needs to take in order to catch up is to expand the HR team's understanding of the business to incorporate business context in everything they do. They need to change their capabilities to align with business needs, especially in the areas that matter such as talent, organization design and culture.

In order to support these efforts at the organizational level, leaders must be more transparent with HR in their strategic planning efforts, while at the same time vocal about their expectations of HR's role in delivering on these strategies. HR needs to be treated as a business president, held accountable for P&L responsibilities and performance expectations as other business leaders.

When HR's perspective surpasses the CEO's

When HR's strategy delivery programs are advanced beyond those of the organization, stakeholder management becomes key. It becomes the responsibility of HR to sell the organization on opportunities they have created. By using the corporate context as the basis for their HR strategy, they can make it tangible for laggards.

HR can jump-start the process by creating "killer apps" (such as leadership development), that resolve pain points in the organization, and gain credibility. Once they demonstrate their ability to solve this pain point, that positive experience can evolve into a more complete strategy conversation. HR now has an opportunity to demonstrate their facility as Organizational Integrators.

Solutions

Solutions are the evolution of capacity in that they're the way the company evolves. Based on the current set of solutions a company offers, it looks to its stakeholders to decide how to own a larger share of the wallet, ever increasing its ability to solve the problems of its constituents, and evolving its capacity to solve those problems in tandem. Solution-based corporate evolution takes an institution from the simple production of a product or service to owning any of the ancillary concerns around it (delivery, training, etc.) and inevitably evolving those concerns to create solutions or products that address these anticipated problems.

Key components:

Stakeholder management, corporate acumen, creative problem solving, market analysis, cost containment, budgetary strategy, resource management.

How it impacts capacity:

Solutions are where we understand capacity in practice. The evolution of a company means the ability to meet those expanding or changing needs of the marketplace, which will rely on capacity. Expanding or contracting, adding or eliminating, creating or destructing—these are the main decisions that are made around providing solutions, and they must all tie back to capacity. Viewing those decisions through that lens means that all people-resource-related decisions will always be met with the company in mind. HR will never fail to drive toward the best results for the company, rather than making choices while wearing the traditional blinders of the HR-process-only mindset. It's an expanded way to make decisions and drive for results that leaves no problem unsolved and with greater benefit to the company.

How to use it effectively:

Solutions are best created with your stakeholders at the table along with strong market data and analysis. Understanding where your CEO and C-suite want to go is the beginning of the creation of solutions to help them get there. Anticipating opportunities to expand service offerings or to eliminate costs are where capacity-driven solutions start to take the company forward. Expanding the role of HR as a valuable strategic partner that drives for results always produces a better way to operate.

Success trajectory:

If HR is in the business of creating solutions, they're out in front of the corporation in a productive manner, leading and creating proactively. Without this mindset, they remain a few steps behind, constantly reacting to decisions made on their behalf. The following examples show the difference between a capacity-driven HR decision framework and one that is clearly standing behind it:

SOLUTIONS

When the CEO perceptions surpass HR:

When an organization embraces a culture of continuously evolving its offerings and services, it can put strain on the HR group to keep up with the pace.

Adopting a solutions orientation pressures the entire organization to evolve products and services continuously, but especially HR. HR and the C-suite must align on the ramifications of this shift for hiring, performance measurement, compensation, training and development, and new organizational model.

Once the strategy is clear to the HR team, HR must be responsible for developing innovative HR processes that build in the agility necessary for the organization to make this shift.

When HR's perspective surpasses the CEO's

When HR's solutions orientation is more progressive than the organization as a whole, they will be called upon to help break through a 'production mentality' in the organization.

Two major ways they can achieve this is through aggressive stakeholder management, and sharing the intelligence that accompanies such insight. HR can leverage this knowledge of the organization to inform solution development. HR holds a unique position of having a 360° view of the customer and the organization. The other benefit commonly shared by high-performing HR teams in these environments is that they proactively lead and engage in establishing change initiatives that are in lock step with the company's markets and offerings.

Since the organization will be constantly monitoring performance against their customer goals, HR groups can look to solutions that go beyond the functional assessment area (like people analytics) to help their organizations keep up, and plot the course for their more traditional expertise areas such as talent, compensation and go/no-go decisions. In addition, they can contribute in more organizational-wide challenges.

Leadership brand

This could be considered the capstone of the four dimensions, as it's completely interrelated to Vision, Strategy, and Solutions. A strong Leadership Brand ensures that the above components are constantly delivered with excellence. The Leadership Brand is the organization determining the character with which those three components will be delivered; it is the high-level thinking that puts the organization and its welfare above any individual pursuits. The Leadership Brand is the "Who" of the four components, and keeps in mind that all individual egos must give way to a centralized, shared demand for success: the Organizational Ego.

Key components:

Team building, cohesion on all levels, egoless decision-making, strong drive for success, 360-degree feedback, stakeholder agreement.

How it impacts capacity:

The Leadership Brand is the way that capacity is attracted, assembled, measured, and rewarded. It is the way that people resources are marshaled toward the overall Vision and remain connected to their part of the larger strategy. It permeates everything from the Talent Acquisition strategy to compensation and benefit design, and it's reinforced in capacity-building activities like performance evaluation, coaching, talent development, incentives, and rewards. If capacity is the goal, Leadership Brand determines how we will reach that goal. It impacts greatly on the individuals in the department who will live and breathe company goals every day.

How to use it effectively:

It is absolutely crucial that the Leadership Brand isn't developed in a silo. The top stakeholders need to feel involved in its development, own it, and evangelize others. You must always question if it's working to your benefit. Take the temperature of those working under it to make sure it's being accurately reflected at every level of the organization. It must be constantly reiterated in conversations, both written and verbal. And, here's the ultimate question to ask before making any decision: Is this true to who we are? Does it reflect well or poorly on our Brand?

Success trajectory:

HR should be the alpha and the omega of the Leadership Brand, so it stands to reason that they should lead the organization in its implementation. However, if the company is focused on the organizational ego while HR remains in its own decision-making silo, HR can quickly find itself scrambling to keep up and deliver on capacity decisions made without its consent.

LEADERSHIP BRAND

When the CEO perceptions surpass HR:

A strong Leadership Brand in an organization begins with expansive thinking about markets and opportunities at the top of the organization, coupled with a high level of organization- first approach that I refer to as an organizational ego. On a day-to-day basis, this translates into a resolute, purpose-driven orientation that relentlessly focuses on possibility, with an eye toward continuously improving results throughout the organization, and generally instills a firm-wide aspiration to excel. Organizations with a strong Leadership Brand aren't just a place to work, they're a place to make better, and it starts at the top.

Keeping up with these lofty aspirations can be tough for an HR team if they haven't engendered the trust from leadership to explore new possibilities and put in place the frameworks required to keep up with the dynamism organizations like these demand.

Without these elements, they'll be continually playing catch-up, or else get painted into a functional corner. Leadership can help bridge the gap in Leadership Brand between the organization and HR by continuously challenging them to be a part of the conversation and strategy, and leaning on them to help track, measure, and implement the next big idea at the organizational level.

Con't

Con't

When HR's perspective surpasses the CEO's:

A strong Leadership Brand that emanates from a company's HR group can make the difference between a good organization and a great one, as it usually demonstrates high fluency with the company's vision and strategy. When the HR team outstrips the organization's capacity to foster Leadership Brand in its organization, there are a variety of ways in which HR can help shape Leadership Brand. One key area can be taking charge of the company's innovation and excellence initiatives, and communicating a sense of the possible throughout the organization.

Obviously, HR represents the vanguard of talent acquisition by demonstrating their ability as owners of this vital process they can also help create generational change by proposing innovate ways to manage talent. In addition, by aligning performance standards, compensation, and advocating for innovative organizational structures, they can shape the leadership brand. Most important of all, however, is to push the organization to imagine the possible at every turn, and put rigor to the challenge of realizing the organization's potential.

Now that you understand the four main dimensions of capacity-driven leadership, let's talk about how to put that framework into practice in decision-making. Here's where the Capacity Framework comes in.

Understanding the Capacity Framework

The Capacity Framework is the universal tool of capacity- driven business decisions. It's the lens through which all decisions are conceived, vetted, and either implemented or discarded. Since all discussions for a capacity-driven business are made with these four dimensions in mind, it's important to understand the impact the framework drives for results.

Each component brings with it a set of questions that takes that dimension into account. When bringing the Capacity Framework to the decision-making table, you will need to think of questions that address that dimension as it relates to building capacity. The Capacity Framework comes to life as it reveals key criteria from which you can make decisions to build the capacity. The questions underneath the Capacity Framework are known as the Strategic Critique, and they bring understanding of the situation to light in each dimension.

The strategic questions of the Capacity Framework

The questions below are just examples to get you started with asking the types of questions you will need to answer when making decisions using the Capacity Framework. Critique your thoughts in this manner:

Vision

☐ To what extent did I use/apply the vision of the company when formulating my own (or our own) particular vision for a given area?

☐ Does this vision reference people outcomes, corporate outcomes, or both?

☐ To what extent did I engage the Executive Team in the development of this vision?

☐ To what degree did I engage other departments or groups in the development of this vision?

☐ When was the last time my team and I actively re-evaluated our vision (last six months, twelve months, etc.)?

☐ Has our company changed its strategic priorities in the past twelve to eighteen months? If so, is it time that we change our own priorities to match? And, have we revised the vision of HR as a result of the changing priorities?

☐ How well understood would I say our vision is? What tools and mechanisms could I use to share the vision and gain buy-in?

☐ Which audience(s) does our vision serve: employees, leaders, prospective employees, investors, competitors' suppliers, others? Prioritize and evaluate how your vision is best suited to deliver on their needs and wants.

Strategy

☐ Have I employed the following to make the best strategic decisions?

☐ Can we tie back any new initiative or call to action to delivering on the strategic priorities? If not, should we be doing it?

☐ To what extent is our strategy value driven versus output driven? Is our work driving value, and if so can we message it clearly?

☐ How often are we checking in to test where our strategy is still relevant and pertinent to the needs of the organization?

As HR strategy is one of the areas that I believe we need to pay most attention to, to enable us to shift from being function centric versus business centric. I have also provided a 'checklist' below that you can use to quickly assess whether when you build out your HR strategy you are using inputs that go beyond the traditional data sources that HR typically relies on. The inputs beyond the first 5 are those that will take you beyond the traditional HR strategy inputs and help you and your teams build out a deeper more insightful view of what is important to the company and where you focus and efforts need to be targeted and prioritized.

- [ ] How do I utilize surveys?

- [ ] How can I make the most of Executive/Leadership interviews and/or feedback?

- [ ] Am I taking advantage of the opportunity for Focus Groups?

- [ ] What are HR best practices, and how am I participating in them?

- [ ] How can I incorporate supplier input/feedback on tools and processes?

- [ ] Where can I receive input from other functional groups (Finance, Communications, Legal, Supply Chain, etc.)?

- [ ] How am I taking into account board feedback and insights?

- [ ] What does my Investor analysis (investor reports, interviews) say?

- [ ] Am I making the most of a Company 10-K?

- [ ] What is the analysis of investor calls?

- [ ] Where is my top five company wide, supplier feedback?

- [ ] Top complaints, external customer feedback

- [ ] Industry reports, benchmarking surveys, white papers

- [ ] Industry articles, blogs, and news reports

- [ ] Conference reports and data, group discussions, and podcasts about industry events

☐ Any other source of information that may be pertinent to my division and expanding my strategy

Solutions

☐ Does this solution directly address a current concern for our stakeholders? Does it anticipate a future need in a capacity-driven manner?

☐ Does the solution take into account the vision set forth by leadership, and does it build capacity around this vision?

☐ Does the solution create a powerful position through which we can create an actionable, capacity-driven strategy?

☐ How does this solution impact capacity immediately, in the short term, and in the long term? Is this in alignment with our vision, and if not, is it time to reevaluate the vision to accommodate this new solution?

☐ Does the solution impact our Leadership Brand? Is it aligned with our culture? Is it the right decision for our people? For our company? For our vision?

☐ Are there complications or issues that will arise as a result of the implementation of this solution? Are we prepared to address those concerns head-on? Do we have the capacity to solve those problems? What is our contingency plan if we run into trouble?

☐ Do I have buy-in from my stakeholders on this solution? Do I have more alliances to build? Have I been honest in my communication around this solution?

☐ Does the HR team have the capacity to deliver on this solution? Do I need to build more collaboration within my own team?

☐ Are there any other capacity-driven business items I may have overlooked? Are they aligned to our goals? Do they drive our model forward? Do they contain cost or have the potential for a strong ROI? Have I brought forth solutions to any conceivable issues where these factors are concerned?

Leadership Brand

☐ Does this Vision, Strategy, or Solution embody the Leadership Brand?

☐ Does this reflect organizational ego?

☐ Will our people resources be able to support this decision? Is this the best thing for them?

☐ Does this evangelize about the Leadership Brand even further? Can this carry our message to an even broader audience?

☐ Do we have stakeholder buy-in on what it will take to implement this decision? Can we get there together in an egoless way, or will this immediately cause fighting or dissent? What is my plan to address such issues?

☐ What is the tie-in to the Leadership Brand with this decision? Does it reflect who we are, what we're about, where we're going, and how we want to get there?

☐ Is this the industry we want to be in? Does this build Leadership Brand or does it diminish capacity in that regard?

☐   Does this attract others to our Leadership Brand, or will it take away from our message?

☐   Does this build shareholder value under our Leadership Brand, or does it challenge it? If it challenges it, is the end result worth any issue, and what is the plan to resolve any problems that might arise?

☐   Is this the headline we want written about ourselves in the news media? Is what we're doing building capacity and possible advantage, or does it challenge our position in the marketplace?

It's through questions like these that the Capacity Framework can help shape an organization that runs on the four dimensions. You can see the power of looking at all decisions through this lens. As an HR professional who shapes your choices through this framework, you'll evolve into a leader who can build entire industries with the greatest vision. You'll develop a strategic mind as well as a strong ability to implement strategy and make solutions-based decisions. This is the playbook of the Chief Capacity Officer; and in my own book, it's the pole position for the plum role of CEO.

CHAPTER 4: THE CAPACITY FRAMEWORK | 95

Utilizing the Capacity Framework

HR professionals are familiar with new organizational models. As I've said before, models for revolutionizing HR seem to roll out every single year. But, looking at things through the lens of capacity shifts leaders' focus from channeling the tools of HR into streamlined pockets of delivery to taking a hard look at how delivery can build capacity to realize company vision. The goal of implementing the capacity framework isn't just better service delivery; it's achieving the highest level of success one can imagine.

Consider the migration to your new decision-making tool as a spectrum, represented in the tables below, along which decisions are made. On the left end is the starting mindset, or the "Low-Capacity" we talked about in Chapter 4. To move rightward along the scale toward "5" would be shifting toward High-Capacity leadership and performance that involves a capacity-centric lens. Consider the CEO through this capacity-driven lens. His or her thought process might look much like this:

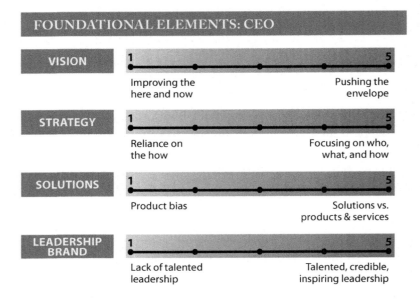

Now, consider HR through this capacity-driven, decision-making lens. Your own thought process might now look much like this:

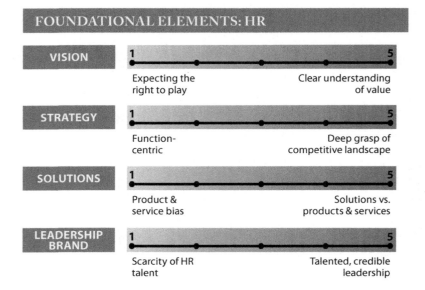

So, now that you understand the evolution of the mindset needed to make decisions from a capacity standpoint, you're going to need better data. The old inputs of information were sufficient for your old way of thinking. This newer, more powerful tool requires you to use more sophisticated information to build your business cases. After all, knowledge is power.

Your old information streams are on the left in the following chart. Your focus now should be on obtaining the vital information on the right, so you can make those all-important decisions with powerful, useful information vital to running your division and leading the charge for positive change for your organization.

OLD INPUTS	NEW INPUTS
Compliance requirements	Board feedback and input
Employee survey	Review of investor calls and meetings for key messages, concerns, and strengths
Handed-down HR priorities set without HR input	
Customer feedback data	Review of company 10-k discussions with the board become part of building the strategy
HR trend data on new offerings and new approaches to core HR services	Focus sessions/interviews with top company suppliers, clients, and target customers
Budget allocation	
Divisional operation plan	Executive team interviews/input
Review with HR suppliers on current and future offerings	SWOT analysis of current HR organization
Silo approach to developing HR strategy (developed by HR for HR)	Assessment "market test" of perception of company brand/image; discussions with strategic recruitment firms, key stakeholder groups
	Review of top performaing companies — (strategy, messaging, talent, etc.) — what sets them apart
	Engagement of other leaders/functions in the development of the HR strategy

With this new data input at your disposal, you're going to have the ability to use the Capacity Framework to make better decisions. Once you've made these decisions, you'll need to be able to translate the data at your disposal into actionable information to bring to your stakeholders. This will require you to contextualize what you know into language your client can easily understand.

To see the company through the lens of capacity, let's look at the evolution of your view of things from not only your own function but also from the perspective of capacity.

HR FUNCTION-CENTRIC LENS		CAPACITY-CENTRIC LENS
Understanding the practice of HR	STRATEGY	Immersion in the overall content of the company
Involvement in organizational design	STRATEGY	Organizational integrator
Understanding customer experience	VISION	Creating stakeholder connections
Delivering people metrics	SOLUTIONS	Harnessing people analytics
Managing employee value proposition	LEADERSHIP BRAND	Creating an impactful organizational brand
Managing change	LEADERSHIP BRAND	Generating change

The start and end points are miles apart. The differences in the capacity-centric skills are depth, complexity, and context. In order to build capacity, you need to understand the total breadth and depth of what it touches. Viewing the company through capacity means a greater grasp of everything it does and stands for. Your reach isn't confined merely to the tasks of the day; rather, it extends to the expansion and health of the corporation, and allows you to view things in the proper context.

Let's look at some of these lenses with a little more depth.

Understanding information vs. understanding information in the context of the company

Now that you know what questions to ask to elevate your mindset and with more powerful data at your disposal, let's talk about the need to understand information in the larger context of the business.

Tom Brokaw once said in an interview, "People don't want you to tell them what happened; they want you to tell them what it means." In order to become a powerful business partner, you must constantly gather and interpret information for your audience. You must translate data into a context that is genuinely enlightening, concise, and actionable for your corporate clientele. When utilizing your new strategic inputs and considering new data, the following questions and actions will help you make what you see usable in the context of the company:

1. **What does the data tell us?:** This goes back to the Tom Brokaw quote. Data for data's sake doesn't tell much of a story. If you discover from one report that the time to fill a position is 120 days and you deliver that information without context, it could prove disastrous for your Talent Management or Recruiting teams. But if you interpret that information in the context of interviews with those involved in the hiring process you might find that the lead time to fill a position is based on a number of variables. For example, it may be 120 days because the hiring involves working across different time zones. Or, maybe the time to fill a position is because it takes the Talent Management team an average of eighty days to get all of the

management assessments and approvals needed to make an offer. Factors such as these tell a very different story. It paints a picture of what the underlying factors are around the lead time to fill a position. Couple these compelling statistics with fact based data, such as the open positions costs one-and-a-half times the salary expense allotted for the position every month the seat remains open, you have a compelling case that's cause for discussion. Don't just deliver numbers: deliver meaning behind the numbers.

2. **Group data into core themes:** Looking at all the data at your disposal, review the information for reoccurring themes and trends. Everything from budgetary overages to the number of customers in a survey who wish you offered a better online shopping experience. EVERYTHING can become a central theme and opportunity to provide context.

3. **Perform a gap analysis:** Do you see performance trends that have appeared over time either in the company's performance itself or in the industry? Are there opportunities that arise from this analysis? Put them into the context of capacity building and present them to your decision-making partners to build awareness and spark constructive discussion.

4. **Identify strengths/areas for improvement:** Successes understood in the right context are great case studies for continued success, and for improving on what's already working. The importance is understanding what leads to the success; that's how you know what to build on. Conversely, identifying opportunities for improvement can bring about the change needed to increase capacity in a certain area of the business. Both are vital, both should be constructively placed into context and brought to the table.

5. **Prioritization (impact/effort analysis):** There's no need to inundate your decision-making partners with all the data at your disposal. Take a moment to prioritize the data by their potential impact on the company, and the amount of effort it will take to act on the data. Decisions should be made with a view to the factors in capacity that will bring about the greatest wins. This prioritization will also help organize the discussion around efforts to bring the most important outcomes to fruition, or to table some things for review later.

6. **Short-term plan and longer-term goals:** Organize your findings around the short- and long-term goals of the company. This requires a focus on determining areas where you can have immediate impact while at the same time focusing on longer-term capacity-building by aligning priorities with future goals.

Building your capacity practice: How to run HR like a corporation

Your new doctrine is "performance first." Your division holds responsibility for a budget and the profitability of its operations and resources. Before you make any call, you'll now ask yourself the following questions:

» What will it really take? Ask this about every task under your purview. Account for every factor.

» Does this action demonstrate the difference between spending a budget and building one?

» Does this help to change the perception of HR from general contractor to architect?

Your new role, as we've said, is to define the "how" and source the "who" of every opportunity—from mergers and acquisitions to global and expansion all the way to managing a global brand. You own capacity in every step the business takes, and with that you will become a builder rather than a simple bricklayer. You now "own" HR as a corporate entity within the overall corporation in which you work.

So, what does that mean?

With this shift in thinking comes fundamental change in how you approach just about every opportunity or challenge. It's this alteration that puts you in a unique position to be an invaluable resource to your C-suite.

From managing the employee value proposition to creating an impactful organizational brand

In the past, HR has focused on the employee-value proposition as a way of thinking about how to attract people and what it's like to work for an organization. In the years I spent at AES, we made many changes to try to improve that function-centric measure to make it more relevant. We finally did develop a really definitive new model that we articulated widely across the organization.

That model was based on broadening the focus to embrace the company's organizational brand: the manner in which all of its stakeholders perceive and differentiate the organization from others like it.

Now, as Chief Capacity Officer, you would say that the employee value proposition is inadequate to your needs. You want to look at more than the work experience at the company and how it attracts talent. We have to think much more broadly. The organizational brand of the company becomes so much more important as access to information becomes easier to obtain and potential candidates display more discerning behavior about what they want and expect from a prospective employer. We need to examine what stakeholders are thinking and saying about us, and understand where there is misalignment or mixed messages in our customer service programs, communications, and media, both internally and externally, that weaken the power of our leadership and employment brand. If the future of capacity-driven business is—as it, of course, must necessarily be—capacity, a dearth of talent is most certainly a big problem. Mixed messages will be easily spotted, and will reflect a disconnect in words and culture of the organization, so it is of critical importance to focus on this.

Go back and look at your organization's people communications. Look at the annual report. Review the investor presentations. Peruse the company brochures and literature. Revisit the internal surveys— "Would you recommend your company as a place to work to a friend or family member?" Use this data to discover where the connections and the disconnections exist.

I went through a similar process and was reviewing many information sources to confirm that we were positioning our company properly. I saw many differences and inconsistencies. It made me think about how we were communicating to shareholders, and that we needed to have a means to constantly update information rather than just in time for the annual report. It's critical to take a big-picture view. You must continue to test ideas against the brand proposition to see that it still holds true.

There is a systemic mindset and a series of supporting practices required for an organizational brand. You have to have both. You have to see how the value-chain happens and design from there.

Modern, company-centric HR departments need to guard that organizational brand. That's all strategic HR.

What's standing in the way of this model being implemented right away sounds a bit familiar:

1. **Vision:** HR lacks vision and expects the right to sit at the table before it's earned it. Before people start listening, HR must demonstrate its unique value proposition, and be a viable producer of solutions worth of an audience.

2. **Strategy:** HR focus is on the functional. Our ability to ask deeper questions and deliver strategic results will move us into the role of central nervous system within the body of the organization. HR becomes the early warning detection system, motivating the body to shift, change, and adapt so it thrives.

3. **Solutions:** The same solutions to new and old problems yield similar results. These new questions will help challenge the status quo, avoiding failure and developing new solutions to thrive in the world of tomorrow.

4. **Leadership Brand:** Top HR talent is scarce. CEOs need Chief Capacity Officers, not operationally focused functional leaders.

From change manager to change generator

Strategic HR means you do not wait until somebody asks you to think about changing the organizational structure or implementing something new. You need to be the one to bring the ideas to the table, to see the gaps, voids, and opportunities; you need to be the one to say, "We should be thinking about this." That's being a "change catalyst."

It comes back again to the mindset with which you encounter change. Do you hide from it in your office, busying yourself with mindless tasks until you can no longer avoid it? If so, you are a change manager only; you will always be a reactive administrative HR manager who never embraces the potential for HR.

If, on the other hand, you can see the need for change coming and cannot wait to map out your own plan for embracing it across the organization, you may be your organization's Chief Capacity Officer. You must not be afraid of generating change for the right reasons. Be a change generator, not a change manager.

I remember a good example of this distinction when I was working with a CEO on the company proxy. It was well written, but I remember reviewing it with the CEO and him asking me why it was necessary to use "HR speak" to explain our compensation process. It was too late to change it at that point, but I resolved to read other companies' proxies over the next year. My team spent time reviewing what made some proxies better than others, we looked at the language, the style and layout and sought to revamp our proxy based on the learnings we had gleaned from our research. We did not wait for someone else to tell us to do it.

The tough part can come when you need to change something that is completely new to you or that you do not completely understand. You have to assert yourself and find a way to understand it enough to carry you through. That effort can give you the credibility to allow you to add value beyond HR. The goal is getting into the position to be the catalyst for the right changes.

Whenever there's a new piece of technology, look at how many of us jump on it. Are we really thinking through whether it's right for the organization? Will it really help things get done? Or, is it just that every other organization has it? We have to distinguish between the platforms that are critical to our company's success and those that are not.

Suddenly we have more powerful metrics across every aspect of the conventional HR life cycle. It's really easy to use the new suites of data to do no more than make the same old job just a little sexier—this might mean bringing a richer dashboard to skills, competencies, and productivity profiles. What is in reality no more than the same-old-people administration now feels smarter and more meaningful while remaining in its comfort zone.

That's a missed opportunity for HR to think beyond our comfort zone.

HR seeks to use technology and Big Data to improve people processes and analytics. We ask the usual questions: How can we pull more data? What new metrics can we track? How can we create new people dashboards? How can we use social media to expand the employee brand? These function-centric questions yield benefits in the HR function but little in the way of corporate impact.

By contrast, the CEO needs HR to provide perspective on how technology and the Big Data it produces can increase the company's agility and knowledge transfer while lowering its cost base.

How will technological change reshape our industries? How can Big Data change the ways we interact with customers? How are suppliers partnering with us to rethink our approach around every aspect of the company? Is now the time to pause and rethink our technology roadmap and our approach to managing legacy systems? What insights and opportunities around costs can we identify through Big Data analytics? These are questions with overarching corporate impact.

And, these are the questions HR must pose—and drive the process toward answering—in order for it to be a true change catalyst, not just a change reactionary.

Being capacity centric is not about models

There are so many HR models out there. Many of them are beautiful models incorporating all of the competencies of HR, and all of the functions. These models are available to you, captured in glorious pie charts. In many ways, these models are static, two-dimensional snapshots. Any of them might be a fine way to structure your HR function, but if that is all you do you will be missing a big piece of what you need.

These models do nothing to create the kind of capacity centric attitude and environment that is critical for being a change catalyst or for guarding the organizational brand. They offer nothing that could help make you the Chief Capacity Officer of your organization. You are on your own there. The models will not give you a roadmap for change— they never do.

Remember Polaroid? It's truly amazing how fast we went from cameras with film to the built-in cameras most phones have today. Most HR models are still stuck in the Polaroid Age, while the needs of our organizations have evolved well beyond the model's ability to offer any relevance. The only way for your efforts in HR to avoid the same fate is to be capacity centric and embrace change.

Stop thinking the same way. Get into the strategy conversation of your company. Do it for the sake of creating value.

Being capacity-centric is about being creative and strategic in business

HR can be a discipline of innovative design; it's creative, not reactive. It's not just about application of models; it's about constantly evolving the model. Other than the CEO and COO perhaps, no one else in the organization has the same opportunity that you do. HR touches all aspects of the corporation. If you have the strategic and creative vision, you have a better view of what needs to be done to succeed than just about anyone else.

HR shouldn't run everything, but HR should be actively engaged in and accountable for pushing the organization. I have had people call me "power hungry" because I would sometimes push things that were outside my boundaries. You have to be OK with the fact that some people will not understand. It's not about power. It's about value. And, if you are adding value, you are doing your job.

As Chief Capacity Officer, your new doctrine is *performance first.*

Five Things to Remember

1   HR and HR professionals must shift perspectives from function-centric to business-centric.

2   Strategic HR leaders think and act like owners of the larger corporate performance plan.

3   Embrace, own, and guard the organizational brand.

4   Go from being a change manager to being a change generator.

5   Your new doctrine is "performance first."

5
WANTED—CHIEF CAPACITY OFFICER
Your Qualifications

I believe that a true HR leader with a modern approach to our profession is in the perfect position to be the Chief Capacity Officer. Such a person already has the big-picture vision, looking forward strategically for the good of the whole company, and is already touching and interacting with every part of the organization.

Becoming a Chief Capacity Officer

As we've discussed in the previous chapters, companies need a champion for capacity at the senior management table, someone who looks at the world through the lens of resourcing. We've come to call this person the Chief Capacity Officer (CCO), and now we'll discuss how this champion runs HR like a corporation, and plays a strategic role in the C-suite.

You already know that no one currently has this job title, but the concept of capacity isn't foreign to senior management in the slightest, so we're merely adding it to the title. Top leadership from Marketing,

Sales, Finance, Manufacturing, Operations, and all disciplines seek to satisfy their own needs through the acquisition and utilization of resources. This is how they reach their goals and the criteria by which their personal performance appraisals and bonuses are measured.

As we have discussed in previous chapters, I believe that a modern, capacity-centric approach is the best way to transform our companies, and that begins with retitling the HR leadership position to that of Chief Capacity Officer.

Bringing big-picture vision to the table along with forward-thinking capacity strategies is the way this position will transform the nature of corporate leadership so that the HR team can assume their position as consummate partners. Everyone wins; all futures are secure.

So, what aspects make a good Chief Capacity Officer? He or she is the one who CREATES:

C	Create the right vision for HR to deliver strategy, solutions, and leadership brand in alignment with the organization
R	Recruit the right people for tomorrow's needs by staying ahead of the growth curve before it starts
E	Explore technology as a means to expansion
A	Advance the tools to measure performance and success
T	Take every opportunity to ask the right questions and know what you don't know
E	Energize all stakeholders by connecting them to a purposeful and transparent organizational brand that drives company value
S	Seek to constantly understand the company at its highest level, holding nothing sacred...including your own role

So, let's explore these themes. You'll need each of them as a Chief Capacity Officer:

Create the right vision for HR to deliver strategy, solutions, and leadership brand in alignment with the organization

There can be no success without vision. It's the cornerstone on which all triumphs are built. Before you can build a successful company, you must be able to conceive of it in your mind. Consider what industry you're in, how you'll operate, where you want to go, and how you want to get there. In order to drive both the HR division and the companies we serve forward, you must understand both these things. Partnering an incredible depth of understanding of HR with equally deep knowledge of the company and its industry is a recipe for success.

You'll need to be a strategic partner in both your understanding of how HR practices and processes can build capacity for the company, as well as the best ways to achieve the strategic initiatives of your company as set forth by the board. You need to know how you can solve the problems of, and create opportunities for, the company you serve. You'll need to be able to give strong counsel and show agility when tough decisions need to be made. For that, you need to have vision.

Vision is more than just forecasting and dreaming up new, fun things to do: it's about how you foresee the company's ability to meet challenges and thrive, with and without resources. Vision in a capacity mindset means finding ways to meet the needs of the company when you have rich budgets as well as serious constraints. You have to think creatively without resources and budget, and major changes require you to think through the bigger details of what needs to be done. Sometimes, the way to develop vision as it pertains to capacity is to get ambitious about how to move the company forward when time, money, people, and other necessities are scarce. Vision is seeing through the panic to solve the problem. It's a must-have for any Chief Capacity Officer.

Vision requires the ability to think about possibilities and potential; it requires thinking outside of your comfort zone, and looking for parallels outside your own wheelhouse. It is probably one of the hardest things to do. There are a lot of good tools and techniques to help people craft vision, and what they all have in common is that they help identify some differentiating factor to aid in solving the problem. For many HR practitioners, vision is often centered on how the organization is recognized as a great place to work. In fact, like many others, it was a vision my team had when I was in my CHRO role.

Looking back, however, I can't help but wonder now if our vision was truly a vision or yet another example of a "me too" approach, where everyone follows what everyone else does with little or no differentiation when it comes to laying out our value. Perhaps our vision should have been to be recognized as the most globally diverse company because of the varied backgrounds and experiences of our people. We were certainly one of the most international companies I had ever worked for, which proved to be of great value in the markets we served.

My point is not to try to teach you how to develop a vision, but to get us all to question our vision statements and ask whether they excite us. That's what a vision should be about. So, step one when it comes to looking at your vision is to ask whether your vision statement makes a statement; is it truly compelling?

Does it connect to your chosen concept of capacity? How does it differentiate you from your competitors?

Most HR leaders (including me) will tell you that they see themselves as a strategic partner, and that they understand the inner workings and goals of our corporations. However, there is a difference between understanding at a sort of Theoretical level and integration of such knowledge into your thinking at the deepest level—total immersion in the goals and values of the company. How to make the shift?

Having vision is an incredible tool. It helps with discovery, planning, and execution. It can put you in front of the competition and give you competitive advantage. But, most of all, it's fun. The challenge for any executive is to find a way to balance thinking and acting at a high level while also remaining out of the proverbial "weeds" on the one hand, and being able to marshal an organization to deliver on the other. Too much time spent strategizing and planning can result in a lack of action. Be wary of being visionary to the exclusion of action. There's a time to plan, but then you must act.

The art of developing a vision is displayed in what you do with it. Vision must be actionable. If you can articulate a great vision but have no clear view of how to achieve it, you're spending too much time focusing on what could be without actually proving you can deliver it. Many entrepreneurs have great ideas, but lack of focus means they fail to deliver. So, have vision but ensure you have focus and a plan of action; that's how you take the concept from design to reality.

When it comes to developing the vision of the HR function itself, the task is to shift from the traditional vision for the group to a higher-level of strategic thinking. Consider the following when creating the vision statement for HR:

> » What is our primary objective—talent, change, process management, leadership, engagement, customer management, people brokerage services? You may find it is none of the above, and that's OK; build out what it is you do, then think about how that can serve the larger corporate vision.

» Ask yourself and your team what you don't want your vision to be by listing what actions and perceptions you wish to avoid. Challenge the typical responses that come to mind. This requires going beyond, "We don't want to be transactional." Go into the actual "because" of why you don't want it. Revise it to something along the lines of "We don't want to be the transactional experts because there are other people who can do that better than we do." "We don't want to be known solely for attracting and retaining talent, because it doesn't capture the full value of what we provide."

» Build out these statements and start to investigate better examples of how to demonstrate value and how to integrate these abilities with the overall vision. The mere exercise of pushing the dialogue and challenging will shape a much richer vision than one that starts from a functional view.

» Another tool is to ask yourself what you would want a *New York Times* headline to be three years from now, about how HR's performance contributed to the growth and success of your company.

All of these exercises are simply ideas, and some of them may not be new to you. They are very impactful if used correctly.

Recruit the right people for tomorrow's needs by staying ahead of the growth curve before it starts

Building a strong, capacity-driven business means having a constant source of top talent who can execute the strategies to keep it alive and well. For HR, this means playing a forthright role in fostering talent while simultaneously identifying and maintaining a watchful eye on high-performing individuals in the marketplace. It creates a constant source of capacity, and it's the cornerstone of the capacity practice. If you can consistently build your internal organization to its optimal capacity and have a source of talent to backfill open seats due to expansion, promotion or other changes, then you are truly winning.

When it comes to building this bench, HR needs to play some rather vital roles:

» **Understanding and anticipating needs:** In order to build capacity, you need to anticipate needs. Immersion has given you incredible vision to see needs before they have to be met. Have discussions around those anticipated needs and also about what budgetary decisions must be made around their fulfillment. Will there be trade-offs? Do you have the talent in-house to meet those needs? Will you have to take on expenses to either train an internal or acquire an external to fill the role? Those discussions can help you strategize about how best to build capacity before it's truly required, which is the highest and best use of Talent Acquisition. It places them into a strategic position of building a pipeline rather than constantly "filling seats" when the head count is down and the hiring decision becomes critical.

» **Pushing back on bad hiring decisions:** avoiding a bad hiring decision obviously begins before the offer is extended, so don't be afraid to push back. Managers feel intense pressure to "fill a seat" when they have a headcount opening, which can lead to a rushed hiring decision. Getting someone in the role is their primary concern, so the pain that comes from a lack of resources can be done away with. Rushing into a hiring decision without fully vetting the culture fit and the viability of the skills they bring to the table is not only a bad decision for the company, it can also lead to a very poor working experience for the person you hire. The time to act is before the offer discussion. Don't resist getting involved. You have built trust within your Leadership Brand, so utilize that good will. Ask the questions no one else will ask. Voice your concerns. Challenge leaders for clarity around the real skills of candidates. Once someone is hired, they become a performance issue. Resolve the problem in the candidacy stage and you can avoid the arduous road of building capacity around a hiring problem. It's worth the conversation.

» **Redeploy existing talent:** The creation of capacity works much like market expansion: you can either make it or buy it. When it comes to making the talent decision, nothing works like the redeployment and repositioning of the skills and abilities of those who already work within your ranks. To realize your vision, your company is going to have to address certain capacity needs. With this in mind, challenge your team to create programs and opportunities to reconfigure existing talent into the capacity builders you will need for the future. Development programs, rotational roles that allow employees to audit other roles for fit, offering roles in organizations to those with similar abilities from other functions (Compensation to Finance, for example) are great ways to build capacity from the inside out. It saves time and inevitably conserves cash and headcount. Constantly challenging your workforce to stretch and grow leads to greater employee retention and a bench of talent that is as versatile as the needs of the market.

Sometimes, you will have to push the boundaries and stretch your ability to build capacity. I had one such experience where building capacity was truly a Herculean feat.

Reality HR, Season 6: How to Recruit 350 Top Finance Professionals in Just Three Months

It reads like the title of a handbook, yet there was no handbook for how to do it. The company had just restructured its financial department. The restructuring was part of a wider initiative to tackle problems that were created by a period of rapid growth. Manual processes, lack of resources had all contributed to the company having to reinstate its finances. To fix the material weaknesses, one thing was very clear. We needed capacity, and that meant hiring an awful lot of people to execute our new strategy.

Luckily, we had a new CFO who understood that this was not a simple resourcing exercise but an organizational build-out. The CFO was quick to engage with HR, which meant we had a true partner in addressing this issue. Our work started by engaging with our CFO partner to design the organizational model that would best help sustain capacity for the future. This included not just looking at the internal structure, but understanding the types of strategic business opportunities we had, what those meant in terms of financial reporting, and what issues and complexities that would entail. It meant our finance teams needed to know more than just finance, they needed to be immersed in understanding the markets we did business in and the requirements that came with doing business in these markets.

We then had to build out the right resource levels and types for our finance function, so it was organized and structured to support the complexities of a global company of our size. It was only by doing this that were we able to build out a map of what resources were needed, where they were to be deployed, and what path would take us to this optimal capacity model.

We had a bit of a branding issue with attracting talent for this new model. Our employee brand wasn't at the level it needed to be to attract the talent we wanted. People had heard stories about late hours, manual processes, and not enough bandwidth. When you couple that with the words "material weakness," we knew people would not necessarily be lining up to come to work for us. We used all the traditional methods to recruit, but we also recognized that this had to be a "build and buy" talent acquisition strategy, that we couldn't simply rely on bringing in all new people. We had to continue to develop the talent of our current people and grow the team already in place.

The overall approach included building out a unique and customized set of competencies with PricewaterhouseCoopers. They had been working to help address a lot of the issues we had, and so had a depth of knowledge and understanding as well as a deep set of financial capabilities that were deemed "best in class" in the marketplace. With their assistance, we not only built out a set of competencies, but a complete assessment process for our eventual five-hundred-person, professional finance headcount located around the world.

We conducted one-on-one assessments and online self-assessments for our existing finance talent, and were able to execute an entire analysis of our functional capabilities and gaps. We worked with our PwC partners to pioneer an online learning toolkit. This allowed our existing finance people to gain deeper knowledge and expertise in functional disciplines through the application of customized case studies, which resonated with the uniqueness of our new model. To further build out our model, we partnered with the University of Virginia's Darden School of Business to build out a finance leadership program for our finance function. We came to realize that it was not sufficient to just have "specialists in their field." In order to be effective, everyone needed to have a level of cross-disciplinary proficiency so there was a complete understanding of the lifecycle, rather than a silo view of their part in the overall finance function. We were able to meet the challenges that came with a greatly expanded vision of capacity for the finance function. And, we created a thriving workforce armed with tools and skills to advance the division into the future.

What really stands out for me is this: what the original need was thought to be versus what the real need was. It was achieved by shifting the view of the challenge from how to hire more than 300 hundred people in ninety days to how to quickly build sustainable capacity for the finance function. If the team had focused only on hiring, we would likely have missed the aspects that were critical to finance the organization's long-term success. We focused on aspects such as how and why the function should be structured in a certain way, in what ways could we sustain the new model, and how our actions would address the short-term material weaknesses issue as well as the longer-term alignment with the company's more strategic goals and objectives.

Explore technology as a means to expansion

The Social Mobile Analytics Cloud ("SMAC") revolution is a sweet spot for HR. It's not merely a set of tools to complete daily tasks; it's changing the way companies operate entirely. One cannot ignore the impact technology has had on all industries across the board, and this is a great, new example. CEOs and IT organizations are struggling to figure out how to capture the value from this disrupter to operating models in a profitable, meaningful way. If HR is doing its job, it is pushing for a wide embrace of this utility to capitalize on these disrupters as well. If we're looking at it as a builder of capacity, the possibilities are endless; and the profitability can be harnessed through creative solutions in workplace organization and cost reduction.

Global markets and teams can operate with little to no cost; whole worlds can be explored without buying a single airline ticket.

If we focus on how it impacts our private little world rather than the whole company, we will lose. Cloud technology is an example of how to view potential disrupters as incredible opportunities. Instead of being a latecomer to the field, we should be getting in front of the corporation and translate its impact before it has a chance to cause confusion in your quest to meet your goals.

Our role as HR is to understand not only how these emerging disrupters are changing how we do our own work as a division, but also how they are changing our overall corporate strategy. This means engaging in discussions with the Chief Information Technology Office not only about how SMACs impact the organization and affect the structure of the IT organization, but also about how they change the operational model for the entire company. We should be leading the dialogue about the need for a SMAC assessment, undertaking a diagnostic to see how and where SMAC impacts our functions, and then become the facilitator to guide the transformation process to adapt. So many people are writing about the impact of the cloud on the IT organization and how it changes both talent and organization models. Yet, the charge to reconfigure or rethink technology divisions is being led by consultants and outside technical experts.

How does HR get engaged and play an active role in this transformation process? We push the change agenda and insist on it being part of the operational and strategic discussion. Start by outlining the impact you see these disrupters having on HR. Use that as an entry point to say that if they have implications for HR, they must have implications for other parts of the company. That's a good way to raise awareness about them.

You can start to engage leaders in discussions about the impact disrupters have on strategy, structure, people, systems, processes, and tools.

Use the Capacity Framework to help your organization map out a process to move from strategy to implementation. These tools and techniques allow you to create a structured framework that you can use to show how HR can play an integral part in addressing challenges and market disruptions that are changing the workplace. By bringing a deep understanding of the business context, you can help your organization to expand capacity and, ultimately, business performance.

A dvance the tools to measure performance/performance metrics and measuring success

As a division that is responsible for both creating and processing many pieces of information, it's important that we're holding ourselves accountable for the right ones.

There are plenty of statistics from which we can draw information, but in the end some are just table stakes. We need to hold ourselves accountable for actionable metrics.

Do we really have the best team in place? Are we spending money in the right places? We should also interpret metrics to make even larger decisions about our strategic direction, such as, "Are we investing in the right opportunities? Are we rehiring in lines that are valuable?"

Analytics have traditionally been where HR has produced reports as a means of saying they are leading. "Look at the dashboards we can produce." Some people love analytics for the sake of showing that we're "doing something." I think what matters are the measures linked to those insights. A headcount report for the board of directors should address the insights you want them to take away from the meeting. Do your hiring practices fit your overall strategy? Are you hiring for where the market is going? Does the plan make sense for the size, cost, and type of the opportunity you're trying to seize? Information is nice, but the insights and context are what matter.

People analytics are about the meaning behind the data. So explain that meaning; use it to springboard into strategic discussions that can lead the company to better decisions. Don't remain focused on the past when it comes to data. Use history to plan for the future. We tend to be very past driven when it comes to reporting, lamenting previous decisions, or holding tightly to past successes. Use that information to drive toward the future instead. In traditional HR, we are selling ourselves short by not providing insightful context with the data we report. In your role as CCO, the bar needs to be set higher. Your role is to provide recommendations, and to do that you need insight and context. Interestingly enough, in every company I have worked with, the "people cost" data provided by HR and Finance were always quite different. One might dismiss that as stemming from different perspectives on the same resource, but think about the inefficiencies that might be created, even if only from a constant need to create "apples to apples" reconciliations. In actuality, the CCO and HR's business-centric "people cost" should reflect a broader and more relevant metric, because it will contain the insight and context necessary to make it so.

Take every opportunity to ask the right questions and know what you don't know

One of the most important things I have learned about being an initial adopter of the Chief Capacity Officer mindset is that I do not need to know everything about everything. The key to success is in knowing what questions to ask and then listening carefully to the answers.

"What's our competitive differentiator?" "What makes us worthwhile?" Those questions go beyond traditional HR tools and processes and drive to the heart of the matter without the need for outside consultants. The reality is that you don't have to bring a firm in to answer the questions you're already capable of asking. As a strategic HR professional and Chief Capacity Officer, you already know the company. The consultant will require a six-month contract to understand the organization before he can answer any substantive questions. Your value comes from a base that is the understanding and experience you already have.

I believe that one of the strongest hallmarks of your Leadership Brand is the ability to take your ego out of the knowledge game. In doing so, you can't be threatened by what you don't know. The modern, business-centric HR team is the only group that can touch, engage, and strategize with all of the various departments and parts of an enterprise. That is where the power and impact of HR and the CCO come from. It puts you in a position to answer key questions such as how the organization can best perform relative to its markets and competition. Approach this in an ego-free spirit of genuine curiosity, gather all the information you can, and then come back with a strong case for action. That's a character trait of many CEOs, but not so much of our top talent in HR.

Interestingly and not surprisingly you do not, in fact, see CEOs coming from HR backgrounds. They tend to come from Sales and Finance, areas that trend toward a broader, organization-wide view of success, accustomed to higher public accountability for all stakeholders. In its usual position behind the scenes, HR has stayed relegated to more internal accountability that doesn't translate as easily to stakeholders. They are not seen as playing a major role in the public arena, nor typically have they have had access to these stakeholders.

Gaining access and credibility is key to our ability to eventually move HR leaders into the ultimate leadership position. With shareholder and stakeholder activism on the rise, and a recent trend of legal changes regarding "say on pay" provisions (informal or legally required disclosure and a shareholder's right to vote on a company's executive and other compensation) both in the United States and abroad, we need HR to become more practiced at stepping out of the shadows and into the public arena.

Shareholders want the best return on their money, and are concerned about huge executive pay packages and bonuses, especially when things go awry. At AES, when "say on pay" legislation was enacted, we had to report on AES executive compensation. I wanted to move forward strategically, and put forward the idea that we contact key shareholders in advance of the proxy going out to let them know what we were planning and try to get their advance views. It resulted in some insight that helped us craft the final proxy. Those shareholders felt that they contributed, which helped us as well.

It was a simple phone call, nothing spectacular; and yet by engaging them early, we were able to accommodate their requests, and demonstrate care and concern for our shareholders. We didn't take it for granted that our carefully constructed plans would be viewed as such by all.

I believe that we, in HR, tend to shy away from the big table because we do not think we have the expertise. Personally, I am not great at finance, but I have the analytical skills to spot trends and inconsistencies. We are all using the same toolbox— analysis, judgment, and thinking skills—and applying them to solve problems.

I will say it again. We do not have to be experts in everything. Asking questions is our way of learning. Sometimes you have to ask questions more than once to finally understand something. Some models or concepts or applications will simply take longer for the dots to connect. If you want to be that business-centric CCO, you have to be willing to really get in there and work hard so that you can add real value to the organization.

You are not going to know everything and that's OK. You may also not grasp the complexity of a situation until you are in the middle of it, but that's OK, too, as long as you stick to the big picture, business-centric view.

Reality HR, Season 7: Grasping the Bigger Picture

At Honeywell in Europe, we needed to rethink our people strategy around acquisitions and restructuring. The complexity came in the form of the various laws and rules surrounding unions and "work councils"—groups made up of union members and senior executives. In countries where the unions and work councils were strong, we had to have a different strategy for our restructuring, because we were limited in our ability to reduce our workforce in those countries. In other countries, we were concerned about increasing the number of employees. By staying within a certain threshold, we would not be required to set up work councils, which had become a legal requirement at this time. The intricacy of a "European strategy" became something that needed to be conceived, implemented, and monitored from the broadest perspective possible, not stuck somewhere in an individual foxhole.

Energizing all stakeholders by connecting them to a purposeful and transparent organizational brand that drives company value

It bears repeating that creating a plan for HR is absolutely vital. A business plan means that the utilization of the tools of HR must meet certain performance goals. They must support the ecosystem of the business by creating and maintaining the capacity for the company to thrive. Incorporating the corporate goals into HR's own performance metrics ensures its goals are better aligned and driving for the right measures of success that will move the company forward. It also gives you a tool with which to galvanize the stakeholders to your cause. You cannot involve others in a great plan that only exists in your head. Build a plan of performance and delivery for yourself, and then set your sights on gathering others under your banner.

Traditionally, we, in HR, tend to come at goal setting from a functional lens, measuring success in antiquated ways. We created performance-measurement tools, scorecards, surveys, general walkabouts, and recruiting strategies that showed we knew the practice of HR; but the complaints remained the same: we lacked context or understanding. We were myopic in our planning, delivering HR tools that were great by our standards, but didn't translate to business needs. We didn't know how to drive business results with our instruments. By viewing things from a capacity mindset, we can look at the overall goals and plan how to transform the company through the right skills and abilities. We share metrics and data, and apply our tools alongside our managers to help them achieve their goals. Our ROI is aligned to the profitability of our clients. We know how to help them win because when they win, we do as well.

Strategic HR leaders think like business owners. They focus on increasing the value of the business. HR, like the CEO, needs to set its sights on the business. How do you do that? By asking yourself, "What are my shareholders saying?" By looking to your top three suppliers and finding out how are they interacting with your business. Your role is to be the nerve center of the corporation. To know how the things mentioned above impact capacity. Play the role of organizational integrator. Constantly ask, "What does that mean for our capacity strategy moving forward?"

Tie all your stakes and measures of success back to the Capacity Framework and constantly check if you're on track with the decision-making framework and initiatives of your company. If the Business Framework and the HR Framework are too disparate, you'll soon be at loggerheads. If you remain in lock step, you can sell your strategies and ideas to key decision-makers with great ease.

S eek to constantly understand the company at its highest level, holding nothing sacred...including your own role

While no one wants to lose his or her job, it's always good to question your utility. If you can consistently prove your worth, it's nearly impossible to eliminate you. Traditionally, HR leaders have tended to look for solutions, benchmarks, and best practices from our own division to show growth and success: but in reality we need to look around to incorporate best practices and success metrics from other departments and even other industries. It's the difference between silos and expansive thinking, and it helps you look at your own utility and measures of success from a much larger perspective. Constantly figuring out what our competitive differentiation is going to be, asking questions about how we are growing our interests, entering the discussion about the identification of customers, new offerings, new competitors, changes in the market—all of these should directly impact our own purpose and how we drive for results.

Over the years, I have become more and more convinced that the key to success in regards to capacity building lies in simplicity and not complexity. I can now look back objectively at the numerous HR tools and processes that I have been involved in shaping. At one point in my career, I am sure that, like most, I thought that the more tools I provided, the better the resulting process would be. So, if the performance appraisal system could provide a hundred ways to show the data, provide reminders and follow-ups as well as produce graphs and charts, the tool would be better. But, I have learned that less is more. The biggest successes and value come when you make something easy to use, simple, and without seldom-used bells and whistles. If you were to go back and examine which of your HR systems and processes are truly being used, it might give you a very telling picture. I am a firm believer that we need not get carried away with our functional brilliance, and instead ask if our customers could live without some of what we've built, and more important, if they really want it.

We need to look at the performance of HR like all other divisions and measure ourselves on financial performance indicators, growth, and innovation. We need to constantly look at our cost structure and ask if there are different ways to provide our services.

We may, in the future, need to think of ourselves as smaller brokers of services who bring in experts where needed. We must question whether our model needs adapting. Along with enhancing existing solutions, we should think forward to identify new solutions to old problems.

Companies typically have three or four key levers they consider to be the overall value drivers, things that move the needle. For HR, it would be typical to expect a focus on cost management since people costs are one of the biggest expenses for a company. Our challenge must be to find ways to manage those costs effectively, ensuring that the value our cost structure produces matches or exceeds our goals and objectives. In practice, that can mean identifying innovative compensation practices, providing analytical data that give insight as to whether our departments are managing their own costs effectively, assessing a more efficient link between performance and compensation, and looking at new and different organizational structures to discover more efficient models of cost, productivity, and talent.

A great example of this evolution in problem solving is General Motors. As part of the government bailout, GM was in serious need of restructuring; so rather than hire a CHRO from outside, they chose Mary Barra, a talented leader from Engineering, and placed her in the top HR role. Internally, many viewed this as the end of her career—why would anyone want to run HR, a second-class citizen as compared to the rest of the organization? Externally, people in the HR community were asking why someone with no HR background was placed in the top role during a crucial, turnaround situation. How could she possibly be successful?

The reality was that she was extremely successful, so much so that in 2013 *Bloomberg Businessweek* ran an article about her entitled, "GM's Next CEO May Not Be a 'Car Guy.'" But, the headline in my mind should have been about how leading HR prepares you for the role of CEO; it was her stint in HR that made her a leading contender for the top spot. This happened because she approached the HR role with a fresh perspective. She saw that the organization had far too many management layers, and embarked on a major restructuring. She looked at things with a critical eye, and dismantled sacred HR processes and tools. In their place she worked with the team to implement programs and initiatives that positioned the organization where it needed to be. It was not her engineering background that made it possible for her to succeed; it was her depth and understanding of value, effectiveness, and efficiency. It is not outside of any HR leader's grasp to approach his or her role in the same way: with a true understanding of the top value drivers and a corresponding knowledge of where and how to deploy HR expertise to deliver on them.

As I said in Chapter 2, you have to be prepared to lose your job every day.

Chief Capacity Officers are willing to have tough discussions. You must be candid and transparent, put your facts on the table, be clear about your hypothesis, and own it as your point of view—then own the consequences that go with it.

Start with a really deep understanding of what the company is about, the real strategic vision and direction, from very different perspectives. You need to get to the point where you can anticipate the thought processes of the CEO, the Board of Directors, the company's key investors, employees and any other significant stakeholders, including your customers. Immerse yourself from all angles. Understand your organizational brand. Know your subjects cold.

If you have not already done so, change your perspective from narrow to broad. Think big picture. Always try to place yourself at the 30,000 foot level so that you can see all aspects of an issue. Think organization-wide about what capacity involves. It's about more than people initiatives. It starts with dynamics. Your role encompasses all functions. Your job is not to own or lead them, but to build the capabilities that the organization needs from them.

In this chapter, I have tried to show the mindset and vision needed to effectively run a modern, business-centric, HR operation, and at the same time vastly increase your contribution to the organization's overall success.

Ultimately, your goal as your organization's Chief Capacity Officer is to become someone who CREATES. And, that starts with harnessing the power of the capacity-driven framework to shape your own destiny.

Five Things to Remember

1   Companies need a chief at the table who sees the world through the lens of resources and capacity—the Chief Capacity Officer.

2   As CCO, you do not need to know everything. The key is knowing what questions to ask.

3   Change the game by how you think about it. If necessary, take a different tack.

4   Go beyond the limits of simple "people metrics." Use vision, context, and insight to really understand the dynamics of your organization.

5   Ultimately, your goal as Chief Capacity Officer is to be someone who creates capacity.

6

WIN THE GAME BY CHANGING THE GAME

The CCO as Capacity-Centric Leader

Now that you have these tools, let's talk about how to influence your stakeholders, starting at the top.

You understand the tools used to make decisions about capacity and have built a toolkit to deliver the results. Now that we've understood the tools used to make decisions about capacity, and built a toolkit to deliver the results, let's combine the two as a final set of tools: the ability to drive a company toward capacity.

Build alliances and turn naysayers into HR fans

I'd like to offer a story from my own experience to illustrate that this concept of converting an adversary into an advocate is entirely possible.

Reality HR, Season 8: The Elevator Story

In my career I have found myself in many roles where I had to learn a lot in a very short period of time. When senior management was decidedly old school about HR, that usually meant added stress.

In one case, I was working with a senior executive whose background included senior roles in legal and finance as well as in running large business units. He was smart, but had a short attention span, and I knew when I was assigned to work with him that I would have my work cut out for me in getting him interested in the value the HR and I could provide. My first opportunity to engage in a conversation with him was in an elevator. I took that moment to make a stand, to make myself known. Confidence in what you bring to the table is critical for credibility and authenticity. Knowing him not to be a huge fan of the HR function—he saw it as unnecessary or at best a burden—I wanted him to know that I knew what he thought, and that I saw it as my responsibility to make him change his mind. I have a tendency to be pretty candid, so I confidently conveyed to him that I was delighted to be his new HR partner. He looked at me with a grimace. His only reply was, "Hmm." To gain his respect, I knew that I needed him to see that I understood business, the numbers, the challenges, the risks, and the opportunities. My initial conversations focused on these very things, not the usual HR stuff he was expecting. He began to see that HR's contribution was not just simply transactional, but strategic.

A year later, we worked together to transform and redesign his entire organization, eliminated $3 million worth of cost, and created a definite partnership with his organization. The HR practice was consistently invited to the table on all decisions.

How did this happen? By our demonstrating a depth of understanding of his department: the market, the competition, and the cost drivers. While he was being pushed by his leadership to reduce headcount, I was on his side, arguing the futility of reducing heads as the right solution to achieve cost savings.

My argument was simple, of course I could help taking out a hundred people, but the reality was that I could achieve the same cost saving by taking out ten very expensive leadership positions. The outcome in terms of savings was more or less the same, but the impact of reducing 10 versus 100 people had very different ramifications for the company.

It was a two-way partnership: I learned a considerable amount from him and the other business leaders about running a business and what that takes. Today, he and the other business leaders remain firm friends and mentors.

In order to win at capacity-driven business, you need to be able to prove worth and build alliances with stakeholders, which means having fans.

Key tasks:

Be direct

» The first thing, from an individual perspective, is to be able to articulate what you do very clearly and succinctly, as you would if you were making an elevator pitch. That is, you should be able explain in thirty seconds what it is you do as an HR professional, why it is you do it, and articulate the value you deliver. You need to be able to very clearly and very credibly articulate what HR does as a whole, too.

» You must strive to always be deliberate in the delivery of all messaging. Own what you say, be willing to back it up, and stand alone, if necessary. Come to every discussion with the strength of your convictions. Wavering will cost you credibility.

» The ability to build capacity sometimes means tough discussions about those things that cripple it. Be ready to touch places that are sensitive to some managers, and stay the course. It may take more than one discussion to persuade someone to let go of an old beloved process or to embrace change. Choose your approach (for example, using harder vs. softer speech) according to your audience, but be consistent in your delivery and work to bridge understanding.

Don't be intimidated by an initial lack of trust

» If you're coming in from a position of not having proven yourself, don't be discouraged or intimidated. You have the opportunity to build your own brand through playing the role of true partner.

» Take the time to really understand where their pain points are, their opportunities, what it is that's driving them, what they need to be successful, etc. Then, you can identify the critical parts of your toolkit you can bring to bear on their needs.

» Demonstrate how you can take something off of someone's plate, or how you can help them think very differently about a problem. This helps to build credibility and engagement.

» It's about not walking away the first time you get knocked back. They may initially say, "Yes, that's all very well and good, but we're not really interested in going in that direction." You must be willing to continually go back until you find the right opportunity. It might not be the one you think is the most strategic, but if it helps to build the relationship, then it's important to use it as a lever to open the door to further engagement.

Deliver on your commitments

» Demonstrate unwavering commitment to deliver results. If you've promised it, you'd better deliver it.

» Have the self-awareness to look critically at your HR processes and services, and not be defensive or protective about them. That's being willing to think outside of the box. Consider how other operational models or ideas can be applied to HR to create innovative solutions. The right answer might not be the one that immediately springs to mind from your own experience.

» If there's going to be any delay to delivery, explain the situation up front, revise your delivery time frame, and stick to it. There are rarely multiple opportunities to regain trust once it's broken.

It's not about a seat at the table: capacity *is* the table

You've been given the tools to participate in key discussions, so ensure that every conversation has a purpose. As an example, you'll want to ensure that you start the talent discussion with the board and CEO, bringing your well-thought-out, capacity-driven point of view, constantly positioning your statements from the standpoint of capacity. You will consistently prove your value if you drive for results from this place of strength, approaching things from your conviction that all things trace back to capacity.

Key tasks:

Ask if you have the right people in the right place. Building a capacity-driven business means positioning people effectively to achieve the goals of the company. Talent discussions need to be constant, not a static, annual event. Our marketplace changes in a matter of minutes, so you should be reassessing on a more frequent basis.

Make talent management part of the board meetings. ALL of them, not just once a year. It will fundamentally change the discussion, and raise the visibility of any capacity issues way before they become critical. Bringing the talent management discussion to every board meeting ensures that top performers remain on the minds of the C-suite and above, and it flags performance and capacity concerns at a high enough level where decisions can be made swiftly. Everyone wins when the capacity discussion is top of mind at all major meetings. There also needs to be talk of outside targets to build leadership capacity at these meetings. There's always a premium on talent. Those who act swiftly and remain consistent in their recruiting efforts reap the greatest rewards.

Board members need to mentor the top leadership. Pairing board members with top leadership can be easily achieved by assigning individuals based on the expertise of the board member, and the needs of the leadership team member. Board members are now more involved in the growth of their investment, and the performance expectations of the top leadership will be elevated.

Get away from the "someone has to be in a role two or three years before you move them" article of faith. The agility to move people around makes the company more apt to meet the needs of the marketplace. The trade-off is between continuity and marketplace agility. When opportunities arise, look at performance, not static promotion schedules. Your workplace will be known as one that rewards for performance, and your capacity will only grow as a result.

A further note about the mindset around more rapid talent development

Think of bringing the talent discussion into every annual budget planning cycle, and engage in assessing what the budget priorities require.

Rethink the leadership development "hamster wheel" that keeps us going round and round with the same kind of leadership development programs. Think about using the board expertise in a broader context. Could they be the best source of mentorship for your talent?

Is there a way to connect talent development with social impact by redesigning how you think about leadership development? Understanding some of the bigger picture drivers outside of your company, but affecting the corporate landscape can help you innovate your people practices.

Consider for a moment how the social impact dialogue is taking on a voice of its own today. Is there an opportunity for HR to be innovative in connecting social impact and leadership development? Is there a way to work with foundations, nonprofits and other organizations on projects/initiatives that build leadership capacity while, at the same time, strengthening company brand image? Is it time to put traditional leadership training models to rest and connect leadership development, brand, and social impact together?

Drive leadership toward the Capacity Framework

We spend endless amounts of money on competency models but there are only three or four major components that drive the development of capacity. Let's get away from complex competency models, and make things simple and effective.

Rethinking the competency model approach in the same way that you now think about capacity encourages valuable discussions. It causes you to consider redesigning your processes, and think about how much value you're really gaining from the cost and effort that is put into the tools and processes you have in place. Step back and ask where the real capacity-building value is. Maybe a one-size-fits-all model no longer makes sense, and you can redefine what leadership success means, focusing on developing tools and resources that capture these new performance measures in an impactful and useful manner.

Key Tasks:

You have permission, as one of the executive leaders, to require a justification for anything. As the owner of capacity, you have the right to question if something isn't working. Just because it's been there forever doesn't mean it needs to be there any longer. Use the Capacity Framework to ascertain if something has outlived its value, and then drive toward better alternatives.

You need to be in the game asking questions when it comes to the money spent on personnel. Do new models make sense? Should we spend this money here or there? Capacity means putting the right resources in place to get the best ROI. If it's worth the money, justify the expense, but if it's not worth the money, say so.

When trimming the fat in both people and processes, you have to be willing to look at your own organization and make some tough calls. Figure out the best allocation of your own spending, align your budget with how you intend to reach your own vision along with the company's. If you see excess, you have to follow your own mantra. A cut in your own budget could free up capacity somewhere else. Be selfless and adopt the organizational ego around having tough conversations within your own function.

Understand organizational readiness. You have to know the appetite of the organization for what you're bringing to the table, so ascertaining the company's ability to embrace change will help you plan your strategy. If you move full steam ahead and find that no one is with you, you lose credibility and value with your customers. Be methodical and consistent in your approach. You can't go too fast or you'll get burned.

Bring your leadership team to the Capacity Framework way of decision-making. You're using a framework tool that can be applied to any strategy discussion to explain how things fit together and how to make the best decision, but you almost want the transformation to a capacity mindset to be unnoticed. Adopting the Framework on your own and having successes will lead others to ask how you're doing it. Gradually roll the concept out through proven results.

The Capacity Framework is a dialogue tool that allows HR to bring departments together to ascertain strengths and weaknesses, and create interunit dialogs to foster links that bring people together. The Framework also sparks a conversation around where HR can best serve and lead, understanding where all the parts come together, and what's needed to move forward and win as an organization. It gives you a plan for strategic dialogue built on what you can do to bring the company to full capacity. Use it, and then evangelize about the capacity-driven mindset throughout your organization. Bring everyone to your side of the table.

The CEO and the CCO: forging the bond

In some cases, cementing this relationship is really hard work and takes a lot of persistence. While you're able to build some rapport on a personal level, you must build a strong relationship where you're seen as a key advisor in their decision-making process. You must continually bring capacity to their attention, particularly if you can use it to address the issues that keep them up at night. As the owner of capacity, your job is to grow that capability for the corporation as a whole, and you should ensure that your CEO's vision and the one you've created are in lockstep in order to maintain that strong partnership you work so hard to foster and maintain.

Key Tasks:

Address the talent issue for them in a way that they want, meaning tackle the big concern that "we're not doing it right." It's been said that great CEOs spend 60 percent of their time on people matters, but we know it's not true that they do it themselves. They surround themselves with people who can provide them with insights; they leverage their talent to help them understand what's going on in the organization. One of their biggest concerns in regards to people resources is whether or not the organization is defining and leveraging the right talent, and whether the supporting talent processes are effective. Constantly address your CEO's concerns proactively by framing your discussions in the language of the Leadership Brand. You must show that your capacity-driven decisions make this a priority.

Your personalities really need to click. There needs to be some connection there; if the two personalities are completely disparate, you'll eventually reach an impasse. Work hard over time to build a strong bond; it doesn't need to exist originally, but you can forge it over shared passions.

Continue to educate your CEO on HR. Understand their agenda, what keeps them up at night, and anticipate what will keep them up at night, and constantly educate them on how HR can resolve those issues. Use the Capacity Framework to build vision and strategy around their concerns. Make their job easier by forging ahead and creating opportunities where they didn't know they existed. Anticipate needs, and you will become an invaluable part of the CEO's day-to-day operations.

Be willing to be candid and constructive—suggest solutions to the problems you identify. You must be willing to stand your ground if you disagree with your top management as well as honest enough about own your opinions. Stick to your guns if you believe it's the right thing to do. Strength of conviction is a hallmark of top leaders. But, once you understand you've been overruled, concede the battle, and get on board with the company's direction, shifting your capacity-focused lens to finding or preserving the value in the chosen course of action.

Be persistent with your CEO. Don't wait to be invited to the conversation. Seek out opportunities to do the inviting. Look for opportunities, the gaps or areas where you believe the organization could do something differently or better, and engage in a discussion about why you think what you do. Explain your ideas about what ways to tackle it, be willing to build a case around your proposition, and connect it to the concerns and priorities at the forefront of your CEO's mind.

Creating change, garnering resources to change the game

This is a vital part of building capacity. It involves influencing and understanding your market, building stakeholder relationships, and driving people toward the Framework. Stakeholder management is the name of the game when it comes to building capacity. If a department feels threatened, or if you sense resistance, you have to be able to maintain that relationship in the future, so you must pick your battles.

If you disagree and your opinion has been clear, you have to follow that train and not sabotage it: DON'T be the HR back channel. Support the company, and get on board. Own what you say. Don't become one of the political players by saying one thing with the CEO, and then using back channels to gain the support of others. The biggest credibility factor that you bring to the table is your integrity, which you cannot compromise.

Back channeling damages your reputation, your brand, and the brand of the HR function overall.

When you are good at what you do, many others may be threatened by your influence and power. You may need to be aware and conscious of their feelings, but do not get drawn into political games. It's a dangerous path. Ensure that you surround yourself with people you trust. Your team is an extension of you, and if the team is dysfunctional or has hidden agendas, you will be setting yourself up for failure.

There's a perception that HR doesn't need to be involved in confidential discussions. It's not a lack of trust; it's that they're not considered to be a vital part of such conversations. Challenge that perception every chance you get.

Building board member rapport

Chief Human Resource Officers (or Chief Capacity Officers) can gain much experience and insight from simply working with and being around board members. Do not miss the opportunity to soak in as much as you can. I was lucky to have the opportunity to work with the chairman of the board and others. I gained tremendously by listening to the questions they asked, watching how they interacted and built relationships, and noting what things they considered to be important and why.

Taking advice and being open to what they have to offer is a missed opportunity if you view the relationship with the board as no more than you providing the HR overview, or simply being the functional expert. I confess that this was not obvious to me as I stepped into my role as CHRO, but grasping that role's value and understanding what you can from these interactions is important.

If you have a strong relationship with your CEO, you can go into board meetings with a difference of opinion, and have a fruitful dialogue without either of you losing credibility. This allows open discussions to take place with the board.

Capacity and the customer

With the rise of social media, the customer is no longer just the internal customer of the client groups HR supports.

Instead, it could be anybody within the realm of operations, and that includes the inevitable external customer. We used to think that the CEO was the only audience we had to please, but that's not being good at your job. That's playing a game of politics, which can only take you so far. Basing your track record on credibility and results is the only way to an impressive history of success, and the only real way to please the right people. Demonstrate your acumen, and the world is your oyster. Don't tell them you can do it; show them.

Key Tasks:

View your stakeholders as investors. Everyone who comes into contact with your products and services—from prospective employees, suppliers, social media followers, to your internal employees—should be viewed as investors or stakeholders in the future of the company. Building capacity is no longer about internal decisions; every aspect has the potential to affect it. You must make your decisions from a more global view. We've seen companies fall to pieces with an ill-advised social media release, causing great challenges to their capacity models. Everyone should be considered in discussions, no matter how far removed you believe they are from the end result. Not only is the company our client, the end users and external customers are as well.

Navigating rough times

This is when you become a real leader. Your job as a top manager is to shield your team from the roughness, but be transparent enough so they understand that it's not all wine and roses. Be truthful, be caring, and deliver updates when you can and when it makes sense. Anticipate questions, gather trust by having group discussions regularly and individual conversations when necessary. You have a leadership role to play within the organization in general. Help to manage the inertia and gossip that happens when hard times come around.

Key Tasks:

You can't take stuff personally. People tend to be terse in communications during rough times, and may not always have the nicest tone when dealing with you. That's not the time to fight a personal battle. The organizational ego must be top of mind at all times. It's not about you. Stay the course, maintain a global focus, and take the higher ground.

A lack of resources doesn't mean a lack of capacity. Get creative and look for new sources of bandwidth for your organization. Refocus internal resources. Make cost containment an incentivized activity. Whatever it takes to get through rough times is what needs to be done, so think outside the box and get those creative juices flowing.

Hold nothing sacred. In addition to celebrating quick wins, you'll also want to ask hard questions. Is a redesign in order? Do you need to release some hallowed ground or antiquated practices for the greater good? This is the time to take sacred cows to the table and review their usefulness.

You need to be resilient and get good at understanding stakeholder management. It's not about good communication skills and teamwork alone. It's about being confronted with competing stakeholders with different agendas and needs, and you'll have to be able to navigate through the noise to be effective in the role you are being asked to perform.

Celebrating successes

This is truly the best part of the job; and in a capacity-driven business there's bound to be a lot of it. If you've overcome great obstacles, you can go back and laugh at old war stories, and really build some camaraderie around coming through rough periods together with your organization. With all challenges come great successes, and if you handle them the right way, you're able to have many more.

Key Tasks:

Look back to where you started. If you ski, you know the moment where you've tackled a particularly difficult hill. When you arrive at the bottom, you look back and marvel at what you've been able to do. This is key to success. Look back at where you started and look at where you are now. You weathered the storm and have great results to show for it.

Take inventory. This is a great time to lay the ground- work for similar successes. Did you change a process to good result? Did you break new ground? Take notes and recall this example in the future. Also take note of things you would do differently. It can be the difference between repeating a mistake and implementing a flawless capacity-driven business practice.

7

HR'S IMAGE PROBLEM
Changing Perceptions, Securing HR's future

I want the CEOs of tomorrow to rise through the ranks of a modern, twenty-first century HR department to assume the role of Chief Capacity Officer, and then rise to CEO. It is my belief that the broad scope of experiences and successes in HR make them the best choice to lead the organization.

Take ownership: the negative perception of our division

With our eyes on the prize of leading the organization, and all the exciting challenges that await us in our new roles as Chief Capacity Officers, we must agree that there needs to be a significant change in perception and attitude concerning the role of HR across the board. This means change must occur in our industry, our organizations, and in the halls of the universities that are educating the talented executives of the future.

The only way the function of HR will survive is through developing a talented pipeline of individuals who can carry the mantle of capacity forward. But, as we charge forth and change to a capacity-driven model, I want to take a moment to address how this negative perception of HR affects our own capacity and our future.

Our first job is to change the definition of HR. This revolutionary change will only come if we, as professionals, are willing to create the revolution, overcome the inertia, and work diligently to change our brand. Any and all incremental changes we can make will move us along the path toward the goal of making HR an indispensable partner in the strategic management of an organization's capacity and resources.

We must first accept and understand three things that will work against our efforts:

1. Most HR practitioners have not developed the mindset and skill set to operate and contribute at the C-suite level.

2. Members of the C-suite do not understand HR's true capability and value.

3. Students in universities studying business are being taught the "old school" definition of HR, and therefore do not understand HR's true capability and value.

The importance of the diminished power of the HR brand cannot be overstated. As it stands today, if you apply the performance metrics of a successful company to the division's current place in the structure of most corporations, it would either face consolidation or become submerged under other functions. You must apply the same principles as you would to any underperforming unit or product, which leads to the inevitable conclusion that at some point its utility will come to an end. Within our organizations, large-scale discussions are taking place about cloud transformation and the effects of the Social Media Analytics Cloud ("SMAC"). And, HR partners are conceiving of other game changers all the time.

While it is true that many have attempted to draw attention to these catalysts of change, no one is paying much attention to the organization-wide transformations needed. The ongoing technology revolution is a game changer for many businesses but few have come to grips with it yet. Why is that the case? Because HR is not a part of the discussion, or if it is, they're being brought in as an afterthought. Where should HR be? Right smack dab in the middle. The acronym should not be SMAC but SMAC IT. Pardon the pun, but the reality is that these changes have such far-reaching effects on companies today. In the face of these changes, there is a burning need to show how HR is vital to capacity. Unfortunately, HR's partners just aren't grasping this yet.

However, we can't entirely blame them. A recent conversation with a partner of a prestigious consulting firm revealed that the firm is seeing a disturbing trend in companies today. They've found that it's not corporate leadership that's averse to innovating in HR: it's HR that is reluctant, risk averse, and narrow in their way of thinking.

I'll let that sink in for a minute.

The consultant further explained that while HR continues to approach issues from a resource perspective ("We can't do that, we don't have enough people"), corporate leaders are stepping up, willing to bet on the risk. They are asking HR to innovate, to step outside their comfort zone, and—hold on to your hats—offering support. Yet, the traditional HR function-focused mindset stops HR from going forward. A senior consultant recently shared her views on the state of HR. I found it to be extremely insightful: "HR is trying to build a green, high-tech building using the same tools and skills it used to build a bungalow." We have not changed our tools, mindset, and capabilities to match the corporate world of today.

Now, let's talk about how the "old definition" of HR derails us, not just in our companies today, but in attracting the talent of tomorrow. We've traditionally taught HR to professionals as comprised of certain functional disciplines, but we've never revamped the thought process to include actual skill. We don't teach our teammates how to develop a business plan for their function; we don't coach them on managing stakeholder relationships. We don't teach them how to discern competitive differentials—the factors by which corporations succeed or fail—and we don't advise them as to what core processes and systems they need to sustain growth. Our starting point for teaching HR should be these Business Management 101 topics. While the functional areas are important, we will only change our value proposition from a tactical and operational bias to one of strategy if we are able to demonstrate skill in these vital areas. It will also mean gaining fluency in the language of our C-level clients.

Don't discount the importance of college students' perspective and their perception of what we do. After all, the students in business schools are the CEOs and talent of tomorrow! Their understanding of our utility can be the bridge to exceptional partnerships or an obstacle to building consensus.

I believe that initiatives like this book will begin to address these hurdles. And, while those currently in HR can begin to change the upper management's perceptions of HR's role directly through their actions, it's also important to change the way we prepare those studying for careers in business. This ensures that all will understand the changing role of HR and the potential for HR to make a broader, critical contribution to an organization's success.

So, how do today's students perceive HR's role? Do they see it as one of the more interesting parts of an organization and as a desirable career path, or just an administrative function? Are today's most talented B-school students even thinking about HR as part of their career?

Take a step back and look at what continues to be a top concern facing organizations today, or at least one that continues to get a lot of attention. CEOs are asking, "Where do I find the talent that I need to support my overall corporate strategy over the next few years?" This key question will undoubtedly fall to HR as the source of capacity and the builders of the talent pipeline that will sustain the company.

My question to all of you reading this is simple. While we worry about helping our organizations and CEOs find the best talent, are we making the acquisition of HR talent a priority as well? If we are not, then who is worrying about where HR talent is going to come from? Shouldn't we, as HR professionals, be working just as hard to find the best and brightest for our departments? The importance of this should be even more obvious when one considers the "second class" perception of HR's role in most organizations.

If one of HR's main roles is to find talented people to meet the needs of the organization, changing how university students and talented individuals perceive HR matters because *they are a main source of our future talent pipeline!*

For those of you currently within the function and looking to advance, don't feel you've been discounted. There are loads of people in HR today with the capability to do more, and we must view them in the same way as we view building a division or product line: we must do what it takes to make it stand apart from the rest, grow it, and consistently improve it so it attracts talented, creative individuals. This means that we need to practice what we preach.

Hold a forum that brings together early-to-mid-career HR people, and have them shape and develop the career development roadmap. Engage those with passion and a thirst for learning. Learn first hand what they need to thrive, not what we think they need to do for HR. Ignite the debate about why HR is the missing piece in the discussion, and what happens when its utility is underrated versus when it's at the forefront of corporate performance. Bring the discussion to life with real-world stories and experiences, and not textbook theory.

Now, back to the students, the leaders of tomorrow. I would ask universities not to teach HR as an add-on subject, but to integrate it into every aspect of the business school agenda and call it what it is: a capacity-building component of business organizations that synthesizes people and organization while mitigating legal and operational risk.

Create an HR course for non-HR managers that doesn't necessarily teach functional specifics—such as how to recruit, how to lead, how to communicate, etc.—but rather the function integrates into the other functions of the company, and why it needs to be in sync with operations, not an adjunct you bring in when you think you need it. Teach it as forethought, and it will always be top of mind, rather than as an afterthought, which is where it sits currently.

We need to recognize that it does matter what graduates think about HR. As a matter of fact, it matters a lot! We want to have the best, brightest individuals in our organization. We want graduates to see HR as a capacity-centric, leadership role that represents a viable, interesting career option, not just a functional, administrative role that exists merely because of paperwork.

So, what do most students think about the role of HR?

The Mind-Sumo Survey

Let's look at an innovative venture created by graduate students at Stanford University called MindSumo.

My first encounter with MindSumo came while I was attending an HR conference. I had picked up a brochure about the new company, was intrigued by the concept, and set out to meet them at the conference trade show. I found their table and talked to the two young graduates who founded the company. The more I talked to them, the more their concept resonated with me. I even loved the name—MindSumo—and was taken with the metaphor of wrestling with problems to win a solution. MindSumo is a platform that connects companies and students with the goal of providing interesting opportunities for the students to get great experience solving real problems and even make some money. For the companies, the students represent potential recruitment candidates at the same time that they get to make use of the energy and outside perspective of the students to provide essentially free consulting to solve a particular problem. This connection is through what MindSumo refers to as "challenges." Students create an account on MindSumo that allows them to complete challenges posed by companies. By completing these challenges, students can land jobs or internships, and also win cash prizes.

Companies can create their own online profile page, post to a virtual Career Fair where students can browse news and available positions. Second, they can access qualified candidates through challenges—either fun, brainstorming challenges or assessment challenges where students demonstrate their skills and creativity by solving company-related problems.

I loved their passion and commitment to their new enterprise so much that I decided to set up my own MindSumo challenge to find out what today's university students think about HR, and what it would take to get them interested in HR as a potential career path.

I posted our MindSumo challenges and received twenty-five responses. I picked three winners for the challenge. I was disappointed in the responses since it seemed that so little progress had been made in the way that HR is taught and is perceived by students.

The students' responses were predictable in many ways. While it was apparent that many had been taught the more traditional role of HR in the organization, most were keen to share their ideas on how HR must change to be viewed as an executive level career. And, many of their suggested solutions, while confined mainly to their area of familiarity, focused on changing the perception of HR through increasing awareness of it as a viable, exciting career alternative.

There was another reason that the MindSumo concept really resonated with me. I have said that HR needs to be willing to think outside of its traditional box and come up with new ways to bring value. The MindSumo concept is a great example of the kind of out-of-the-box thinking I have in mind. Not only do its challenges give the company help in solving a particular problem, but also they identify potential recruitment candidates. It is a great example of what HR should be doing—thinking of new approaches to things and leveraging resources in new and better ways.

Following are some excerpts from the survey responses:

1. **Business is all about people. HR is all about people!**

"Business is all about the people... Human resources then becomes a critical part of the success of any enterprise. Although it may not seem as important as things like marketing or engineering, ultimately these departments are all made of people that go through human resources. In order to change perceptions about HR, it is important to convey the fact that HR isn't just about compensation, but it is about identifying and developing leaders. Whether through hiring or setting up mentorship programs, HR provides the critical function of ensuring the sustainability of the company through the development of its future leaders. General Electric sees its core competency not in engineering or marketing, but rather in developing top quality leaders, which have helped the company stay alive for over one hundred years. Similarly, the messaging of HR can take on a similar feel, that of developing leaders of tomorrow."

—William Yan

"A company is only as good as its employees, its human capital. In this way human resources serves a vital role in formulating corporate strategy, both in vision and in execution; corporate culture depends on correctly matching candidate skill-sets with the right positions, and it is an art to place the right person in the right position at the right time. Emphasizing this vibrancy is one way to attract the attention of recent graduate candidates. Recent graduates may also be attracted by the concrete skill-sets acquired through entry-level HR work: the ability to meet complex, overlapping deadlines, to handle sensitive material, and firsthand knowledge of insurance (medical, life, and property), business law, accounting, market analysis for a particular industry, or how to calculate salary equivalencies. For business- oriented individuals, working for HR is an excellent foundation for building one's own small business. Also enticing could be a company-specific "HR Small Business Mentor Program," whereby new HR employees have opportunities to learn about other divisions in the company, and work directly with a senior-member executive as an entrepreneurial mentor. In the process of recruiting students to HR positions, some may eventually choose to stay, and instead advance their career in HR, ensuring the future of the department."

—Dena Feldman

"When I think of an HR department I think of a department that is connected to every department within the business. They deal with legal issues and payment, but they also have to work with everyone so you can gain knowledge about all departments through only the HR department. Many new graduates have very little or no work experience in an office environment, so the HR department could be used as a training system to get newly hired graduates familiar with the company, and then placed in the department they feel is most suited to their skills. The best way to learn about something is to do it hands-on, so this would be enticing to new graduates because they learn to be comfortable in an office environment, learn the overall function of the business, and are able to grow with the company."

—*Richard Mathieson*

2. HR is perceived as "mind-numbing"

"Here's the problem: No one hears the phrase 'human resources' and thinks of an exciting, dynamic job with real impact. Human resources means mind-numbing bureaucracy, exhausting amounts of paperwork, and a mindset stuck squarely in the twentieth century. Start off by dropping the name. Let's call the twenty-first century version of HR something honest, but refreshing: People. So, now you're not looking for 'a managing role in the human resource management division,' you're looking for 'a people person.' Which would you rather be? Now that you've broken all the negative connotations associated with HR, you can make it absolutely clear what a people person does. And, what's being a people person all about? People, of course! You want to hire people who love getting to know new people…"

—*Pranjal Vachaspati*

"In order to change the perception that HR is not just merely an office in the corner printing out employment contracts and paychecks for other people, the worth of the HR must be elevated for prospective employees. HR is an invaluable part of any company, and its department employees are vital to the culture of the firm and its direction. HR is responsible for the recruitment of new employees, and the way recruitment is handled determines the success of the team. New talent brings possible change and manpower for existing or new initiatives—it drives the focus of a firm. The competition for new talent is intense, and it is HR's responsibility to wade through the thousands of new graduates and develop a strategy for acquisition. They decide which schools to contact and in which manner. They are the gatekeepers. As far as I know, the HR department is a mystery to many students qualified and fit for the position that otherwise just do not possess any knowledge of the position..."

—Kathy Vu

3. Trumpet the work and potential of HR!

"The fastest way to change perception regarding HR positions for graduating college students would be to change the focus of the job titles and descriptions for entry-level positions. Many of the sought after entry-level positions in other areas of business include terms such as specialist as in 'Marketing and Communications Specialist.' To begin the process of changing perceptions about HR positions set the standard for entry-level positions to be titled 'Talent Acquisition Specialist' or 'Talent Acquisition Associate.' These are attractive titles that would draw interest from a wider range of students considering a career in human resources. The job descriptions need to fall in line with these new titles, show that the most important portion of the job is acquiring and retaining top talent."

—Clark McMahon

"The human resources department is key to the success of any business, not only for maintaining a solid workforce, but also for keeping the workforce interactive. To change the view of HR as the sour old man in the back office, several paradigm shifts are needed... HR departments do a lot of work, and don't get as much credit as they deserve. By showing off the work they do, students will be more attracted to work there. Reaching out through department coordinators and career centers will offer a reliable connection to students, and bringing alumni into the picture keeps them involved and the applicants flowing."

—*Noah Greenbaum*

"To change the perception about HR, I would first target the people who currently have the biggest problem with HR: engineers. The message that engineers want from HR is: 'We are not going to be in your way. But, here is how we can help you.' HR departments can achieve this by taking steps to streamline paperwork, (e.g., sharing documents on the cloud, using simple forms and simplifying the steps of a procedure as much as possible.) Having engineers (both employees and those being recruited) say good things about HR is a great way to spread the word and make that HR department stand out."

—*Cathy Wu*

4. Students need to experience the challenges of HR

"To best market HR positions to graduating college students, I suggest creating HR-specific case study competitions. HR firms/departments can create cases that showcase the intellect and creativity required for the job. Students can be shown that solutions to these problems will affect organizations in many ways. Short of actually working or interning in HR, this simulation is the best way for students to experience the challenge of HR, not just hear or read about it. In addition, firms benefit, as they will see how students can perform in HR, a more telling process than simply asking them how they have performed in the past. In sum, HR-specific case competitions are the best way to increase HR appeal to graduating college students. They let students experience solutions to challenges HR poses, gives firms flexibility in catering to various recruits, and allows for appropriate scaling."

—*Wesley Panek*

I think that in these excerpts we see perhaps the most important thing we could want to see: open minds. Earlier, I said that I was disappointed in the responses. What I meant was that, although they're full of great ideas, they also show the lack of progress we've made over the years in making HR an appealing executive-level career. Not one of them challenged the notion that HR isn't already an exciting field. We have an opportunity to change that by taking note of what needs to change and acting on it purposefully and directly.

Many, if not all of the respondents were more than willing to embrace the new definition of HR and the expanded role of HR in an organization. Many had interesting and innovative suggestions about how to change the perception of HR among students, and how to make it more interesting as a career path. What we need is the support and reinforcement of educational institutions and their faculty members to change the messaging and lesson plans around HR.

These students need to come into the world of business with an expectation of HR as a capacity-centric, strategic voice in whatever organization they become part of. I want those students to see the value in pursuing a career in HR, not because it is safe and easy, but because its challenges are at the heart of building any organization.

High stakes, broad responsibility... no authority

So, even the students have seen it. The expectation is that HR is to manage the people agenda, but only as a limited executor of the strategic agenda. Its impact is limited to what it knows. It's a catch-22 in the sense that the function is criticized as not being strategic, and yet is often not invited to the most critical discussions that drive growth and performance.

The stage is set: a revolution in the perception of HR is more necessary than ever. If we are to move forward, we must think about the future of our department, and that future is capacity. If we stake our future on the exciting prospect of solving problems through the lens of capacity, we can offer powerful career options for not just future generations, but for our existing talent as well.

Five Things to Remember

1   We must make a revolutionary change to the definition of HR. We must create the transformations we wish to see and overcome the inertia we face when it comes to the stagnant, antiquated perceptions of a career in Human Resources.

2   We need to alter the perception of business school students. Our current talent pipeline exists within other companies, but our future lies with those studying for corporate leadership positions as we speak. We must evangelize about the changing role of HR and the potential for a career within our ranks to make for a broader, critical contribution to an organization's success and a challenging, rewarding professional life.

3   Today's students are ready and willing to embrace the new vision for HR, and we need to give it to them.

4   University faculty need to understand, provide instruction about, and reinforce the new messaging around the importance of HR. We need their assistance to make a career in HR desirable.

5   Look for the CEOs of tomorrow to come from disciplines that include strategic, capacity-centric HR. It is possible, and capacity-driven business is the key to that future.

SOME CLOSING THOUGHTS

We've come a long way on this journey through the tools of capacity-driven business. You've learned quite a bit along the way about how to take the tools of HR and evolve your thought processes to that of a high-vision leader. You can look at any situation through this lens and align your decisions to the ultimate goal of building capacity for your company.

As someone who has used these tools to great reward in my own career, it is my distinct hope that we evangelize this message. HR is more than capable of running itself like a corporation, and we're incredibly capable leaders that can transform organizations with not just the tools of our function, but with a deep understanding of the tools and capabilities of our clients. The world is at our disposal. With a deep desire to learn and understand that marketplace around us, we're able to bring solutions and ideas large and small to fruition. We are able to assume the mantle of CEO through our journey as Chief Capacity Officers.

It is my desire that you'll help me evangelize this message, that we are not doomed to the negative perceptions of our practice that have haunted us for so long. HR contains a wealth of talent and knowledge that can be used to move our corporations forward. We should not provide the opportunity for others to perform tasks we are more than capable of doing ourselves. We should be the first resource anyone thinks about when transformational activities are considered. We need to anticipate the need for change and then deliver the next evolution of that aspect of capacity. As the owners of capacity, we should manage that part of the destiny for our organizations and our own people.

It is my strongest wish that the Capacity Framework elevates your career to the highest level you can imagine and beyond. These tools are meant to elevate your position in the minds of your constituents and to help you sit comfortably at that seat at the table. There's nothing you can't achieve with these tools in place. The Capacity Framework is my own proprietary tool that I developed based on my years of experience of what makes for a successful HR function. I would love to connect with anyone who wants to know more about the tool and how they might apply it in their organizations. If you liked the book or have comments, feel free to contact me at rita@ritatrehan.com.

As the owner of capacity, you ultimately control the world of capacity-driven business. The power is yours, the time is now, and you are the right person.

Take it.

!

Seize it.

!

It is yours.

!

ABOUT ME: THE PERSONAL SIDE

The personal me is a reflection of my upbringing, my experiences, and the principles I hold dear. They reflect the who, what, and why I am. So, I wanted to share a bit about me, the family that shaped me, and the colleagues and individuals who shaped pivotal moments during my career.

The quick family snapshot

My father left his hometown in India in the early '60s for England. The premise at that time was simple: he would find work, and once established would send for his wife (my mother) and young children (my brother and sister) to join him. His sole focus was to make a good living to support his family while at the same time supporting the family back in India. (I, at this stage, had yet to appear on the scene.)

My parents' work-life in the early years was all about hard work and ambition. From working on the railways, to being a door-to-door salesman and many other jobs in-between, my father worked hard. My mother was no different, working at home as a "piece machinist." They ended up, before they retired, owning a couple of high-end fashion retail stores (now run by my brother).

The essence of my parents' approach to work and life has always involved a few key beliefs ... you work hard, know that nothing in life is free, your reputation is everything so treat people with respect, ego is a wasted use of energy, and last but not least, learn from those that know more than you.

More importantly, my parents showed us what was possible. If you had determination, belief, willingness to learn, an ability to rise above those who tried to belittle you, and did not allow jealousy or ego to rule your decisions, you could achieve whatever you wanted. Life was up to us and what we did with it was in our hands.

My love for Business

When most kids spent their holidays playing with the other kids in the street and doing "kids stuff", we worked in the family business. I think this is where my passion for business first developed. I did not realize it at the time, but it was those early years of understanding what makes a business successful, from needing to know everything from inventory to customer service to having the right products, that my depth of understanding and passion for business came into being.

Me

So, the personal me in a nutshell—passionate, principled (sometimes to the point of being painful), a lover of the underdog, a fighter, comfortable in knowing what I don't know, constantly questioning to the point of being annoying, knowing that respect will carry you much further than power or status, and ultimately never compromising on things that you believe are important. This comes from knowing that life will always have challenges and adversities. But it's how you deal with them that is important, and that when people doubt your motives, never let it sway who or what you stand for. None of us are perfect, but we all have our talents, and this book is about helping people I hope will use their talents to the maximum value.

TESTIMONIALS

"Clearly, HR expectations and opportunities are increasing. Rita does a wonderful job of translating the ideas of how HR can add impact to practical solutions. By following her four phase capacity model, HR professionals can have more positive impact."

Dave Ulrich, Rensis Likert Professor of Business,
University of Michigan and Partner, RBL Group

* * *

"Many CEO's wonder is this as good as it gets? Rita Trehan shows that it clearly is not, that there are real bonds that can be forged and that naysayers can turn into enthusiastic HR brand advocates. With the many transformations happening in today's workplace; the gig economy, Big Data, IoT, it is not an option for HR to wait around, becoming a Chief Capacity Officer is crucial.

"I find Rita Trehan's book a true toolkit for HR professionals that truly want to adapt to the mindset of those beyond 2020 to unleash an organisation's true capacity."

Nicole Dominique Le Maire, Founder, New to HR

* * *

"Rita Trehan's book is the most up to date, realtime look at the role of a Chief Human Resources Officer across companies. In her easy to read, pragmatic and honest description she acts as a strong catalyst for change. Very simply and eloquently, she captures the strong desire I hear so often from CEO's and Boards on the true value they would like to see from HR. She makes it 'doable' with her endless tips and suggestions.

This book is written from personal experience and wisdom, providing not only the 'what' of Human Resources, but also the 'how' and 'who'. Rita's call to action, her description of the transformational journey needed and her inspirational support and advice will no doubt be a source of support for many C-level leaders. It is a book that should not only be read by HR professionals but anyone who is truly vested in building value in an organisation.

"Rita is not redefining the role of human resources, she is defining what it will take for the human side of organizations to thrive in our modern age. The role of Chief Capacity Officer is exactly what companies need to adopt to get out of the struggle many human resources organizations are faced with today."

Ellie Filler, Managing Partner, CHRO Practice, Korn Ferry Executive Search

* * *

"Rita excellently communicates the need for CEOs to sit up and listen to the role that HR can have in driving change across organisations."

John Challenger CEO, Challenger, Gray & Christmas

* * *

"This book is an engaging, enjoyable and informative read. It will help any HR Leader turn their organizational house into a home. For years HR has been living in the organisation and being told "what goes where". This book provides tools and applications to not only design but help build their organization, starting from the foundations."

Randall Thames, Partner, Aon Hewitt

* * *

"Unleashing Capacity shifts the HR focus from managing resources to managing capacity. Rita introduces an intriguing concept of the Capacity Framework to transform Human Resources into a strategic partner within the organisation. An excellent read with common sense application for any industry."

Michelle Bliffen, MBA, SPHR, SHRM-SCP,
University of Kentucky, HR Technical Team Lead

* * *

"Rita's pinpoint analysis of the role HR plays in businesses is not only integral to the HR function but essential for 21st-century corporations looking to transform their organisations. This book is a great read for CEO's and HR professionals alike.

"Rita offered invaluable advice and support to me in her time at AES and no doubt will continue to do so for C-suite executives around the world."

Paul Hanrahan, CEO, ACEI & Director, Ingredion

* * *

"Rita has a fantastic grasp of how HR can be used to leverage greater revenue and output across business sectors. There is no doubt that HR is the main driver of capacity."

Christine Hassler, Best-selling author of Expectation Hangover, Life Coach, Speaker

* * *

"An ambitious and timely vision for how HR professionals can step up, to become the leaders their businesses need them to be."

Lewis Austin, Chief Customer Officer, SCM World

* * *

"Finally an innovative, logical and refreshingly modern rationale for capacity-driven results that breaks HR Professionals free of the antiquated views on HR."

Paul Hebert, Director of Human Resources, Becket Family of Services

* * *

"In Unleashing Capacity, Rita Trehan challenges HR professionals to move beyond their standard contractual and administrative roles and take a critical seat both in the boardroom, and in the C-suite, as capacity builders."

Joe Raelin, The Knowles Chair of Practice-Oriented Education,
D'Amore-McKim School of Business, Northeastern University, Boston

* * *

"Underpinned by a wealth of experience this book exudes energy, hope and practical wisdom. Invaluable both for aspiring HR executives to think and act strategically, as well as showing CEO's the value they can gain from HR."

Dr Clare Rigg, University of Liverpool Management School

* * *

"Rita's book reminds us that HR is far more about people than processes, procedures and analytics. In an increasingly knowledge and talent driven economy, enlightened HR approaches are vital to achieve sustainable competitive advantage and Rita's practical insights and advice make essential reading for those CEOs who are serious about ensuring their people are their greatest asset."

Kate Cooper, Head of Research, Policy & Standards,
The Institute of Leadership & Management

Lightning Source UK Ltd.
Milton Keynes UK
UKOW07f1955200916

283420UK00014B/107/P